Words For Healing

Pursuing Your Healer - Not Just Your Healing

WANDA ALGER

Alger Publications
Winchester, VA

Words for Healing
Pursuing Your Healer - Not Just Your Healing

by Wanda Alger

Published by
Alger Publications
Winchester, VA
wandaalger.me

ISBN: 978-0-9996752-5-0

Cover design by Jenn David

Additional Resources from Wanda Alger:

Words to Pray By

Prophetic Mentoring Training Course

Moving From Sword to Scepter:
Ruling Through Prayer as the Ecclesia of God

Prayer That Sparks National Revival

Oracles of Grace: Building a Legacy of Wisdom and Revelation

Making Room for His Presence: A 21-Day Community Devotional

Getting Free of Religious, Jezebel, and Leviathan Spirits

Dream Interpretation Audio Series

Table of Contents

Introduction

This prayer concordance is much more than just a book to "decree and declare" your faith. It is a guide to His heart. In every scripture listed, there is an aspect of His Perfect Love that is revealed. By reminding ourselves of who He is and just how much He wants us whole and free, our faith will become steadfast and our confidence in His perfect plans for us will be unwavering. Even when feeling desperate for help, it's in touching His heart that we will be changed from the inside out. It's there that we will find the courage, strength, and faith to override and overcome spirits of infirmity and become whole.

In using this prayer concordance, my prayer is that you will meet HIM. The written prayers are merely meant to be "jump starters" and not just liturgical readings. Feel free to paraphrase them as the Spirit directs you to pray. This is your prayer journal, not mine. I'm just giving you a head start in building your own style of communication with the Lord.

I have written all the prayers in first person, but they can certainly be changed to third person when needed. The goal is to establish a heart connection before anything else. We don't have to command or demand His will to be done. He longs to answer our prayers simply because we are His sons and daughters. Whatever healing you need, whether it's physical, emotional or spiritual – He's the answer. He is your Healer. Get to know Him and yield to His plans. Pursue His presence and lean into His heart. You may be surprised at what He shows you.

Though I personally use the English Standard Version as my choice for study, I chose the New International Version as the primary source for the scripture references, simply because it is the most common.

My Own Story of Pursuit

My husband, Bobby, and I have always enjoyed good health with very few visits to a doctor over the past 35 years. We have always led a relatively healthy lifestyle with very few issues that would indicate any troubling medical condition. But that all changed in 2023. Starting with a debilitating attack of Tinnitus in March of that year, I went through months of agonizing torment, pain, and sleepless nights as we contended for breakthrough. The ringing in my left ear was so loud I had to sleep in a separate room from my husband with both a sound machine and worship music loud enough to drown out the ring. For the first time that we could remember, our decrees and declarations of faith seemed to make little difference in the battle. Even as we rebuked the enemy, prayed in tongues, and did everything we knew, the breakthrough didn't come like we expected. We quickly learned that we were being led on a journey requiring us to listen much more closely to the Lord's directives each and every day. Everything we had assumed about faith for healing was being severely tested. In the process, He was going to finetune our sensitivity to His voice and upgrade our understanding of getting healed.

Thankfully, within the first several weeks, the Lord exposed some tormenting spirits that had come to shut down my ability to hear from the Lord and distract me from my call as a prophet. Speaking on national platforms during this time, I had become a prime target of enemy forces. As we sought the Lord for direction, the Holy Spirit taught us how to stop the demonic attacks and nullify their effect. He told us that our relational covenant and oneness in prayer were going to be key factors in getting my breakthrough. As a result, I was not only delivered from these demonic intruders, but freed from a spirit of fear that had settled over me on the night of the initial attack.

Through the process, I even learned how to recognize the different sound of the tormenting spirits and not just the annoying ring of a physical condition. I still remember the night when I knew the last demonic spirit was gone. The bullhorn that had been sounding around a level 7 in my ear was finally cut in half, and there was no longer any torment or fear attached to it. Instead, a blanket of peace settled upon me, and I was able to function beyond just survival and even get some sleep. Even though I knew I still had further to go for my complete healing, I wasn't fighting demons anymore.

The Battle of the Mind

During this initial phase of my journey, the battle was not only with tormenting spirits but my own thoughts. It was just as much a battle of the mind as it was a battle of the spirit. Those tormenting demons had been shouting in my ear non-stop, and I had to learn how to ignore their temper tantrums and not give in to their influence. There were nights when I would plead with the Lord to just make them stop and His response was always the same: "My grace is greater, Wanda!" He wanted me to lean into Him and learn how to tune out the enemy's voice – no matter how loud it was. Little did I realize how much He was training me in the battle. He was helping me to find His grace and strength in the midst of the noise and fix my eyes and ears on Him. He wanted me to know just how big He was and how much stronger His presence and grace were in the middle of enemy warfare. He told me later that the only way I could overcome my fears was to face them. I learned that sometimes our freedom comes, not because the enemy leaves, but because we stand stronger. This was a core truth that would be tested many times in the days to come and marked much of my journey!

During the few weeks when we were battling these demonic spirits, the Lord taught us how to ask for His direction before every prayer. Instead of always assuming we needed to rebuke and renounce these tormenting spirits, sometimes He simply wanted us to worship. Other times He wanted us to be still and quiet, waiting in His presence. He had already shown us the power of praying in tongues before addressing any attack. Because we didn't always know what to do, we always started by worshiping Him and praying in the Spirit. It was then that He would show us what to do. At one point, He even said to just ignore them! He was teaching us to look to Him before trusting in our own understanding. It was a constant reminder that this was a journey of knowing HIM more than just fixing the problem.

"Trust in the Lord with all your heart, and do not lean on your own understanding. In all your ways acknowledge Him, and He will make straight your paths." (Proverbs 3:5-6 ESV)

Crazy Faith and a Controversial Protocol

Once I was finally free from the tormenting spirits, I could finally focus on the underlying physical root causes of the remaining ring. Even as we continued praying scriptures for healing and declaring God's goodness, I knew that some of my physical symptoms were caused by other factors. I knew that it wasn't just a matter of getting healed. It was a matter of being healthy. There's a big difference!

It was at this time that the Lord directed me to try a controversial protocol that carried some unknown risks. Dr. Bryan Ardiss was just beginning to share his breaking revelations about the use of nicotine in healing long-haul Covid symptoms. I had already been receiving messages and emails from followers who indicated they began to experience tinnitus when they got Covid, and more specifically, after receiving the shot. Though neither Bobby nor I had received the shot, we had both experienced the painful realities of Covid. We had also begun to hear about "shedding" and how non-vaccinated persons can experience the same negative effects of the shot just by being around those who were vaccinated. Thus, I was curious if my tinnitus might be the result of shedding.

Dr. Ardiss reported that nicotine isn't addictive (as we've been told) and that the use of nicotine gum or patches had already been tested and proven to eradicate the harmful side effects of Covid and the vaccine. Through several unexpected conversations (one indirectly with Dr. Ardiss), some prophetic dreams, and upon further research, we felt the Lord gave us the green light to try this unusual protocol. Ultimately, we knew that Jesus was the Healer and that He could use whatever He wanted if we surrendered it to Him (1 Timothy 4:4-5). So, we got some nicotine gum, sanctified it in prayer, and I started taking it.

I share these details because my entire healing journey was one of getting His instructions on a daily basis. It was clear from the beginning of this process that He had something very specific in mind to teach us. Knowing how the enemy was going to work, God had determined to use this battle as a means of us gathering strategic intel concerning the devil's schemes. In walking us through the valleys we would face, He was going to give us tools and insights that would help many others who would face similar challenges. But it would require us putting away any expectations or presumptions of how He was going to work, and pursuing Him on a daily basis for direction. One of the major lessons I learned through this whole process was the importance of obeying His voice, and as a minister who depends on hearing His voice clearly and accurately, I knew I wanted to pass this test!

The other factor that made this journey so significant was that several months prior to me being hit with tinnitus, Bobby had been diagnosed with glaucoma in his right eye. Being an extremely fit and healthy person his entire life, this was a surprise to us and we had already been seeking the Lord on his behalf. He was having increased vision problems, and though it didn't cause much pain, he found his energy being depleted and an increased lack of physical strength and stamina. Thus, for the first time in our marriage, we were both experiencing physical issues beyond the norm. I also began to realize that what we were experiencing was no "coincidence." A pastor's vision was being attacked and a prophet's hearing was being threatened. We knew that this was a battle of both body and spirit. So, we set ourselves to partner with the Holy Spirit in this walk of discovery and breakthrough.

As stated before, we knew that our faith was being upgraded and deepened in this journey. We had both already been operating in a gift of faith throughout our entire marriage, seeing God do miraculous things in our finances, family, and ministry. But now that we were both facing physical challenges, we needed to apply our faith to our healing.

Surprised by the Spirit

One of the most surprising lessons in this came after I took my first "dose" of the nicotine gum. What happened upon my simple act of faith will forever be imprinted in my soul and spirit. Five minutes after I started chewing the gum, the Holy Spirit came upon me so powerfully, I fell to the floor in my living room and was overcome by the joy of the Lord! I was totally shocked at this unexpected visitation. After weeks and months of wondering if He was really there in the midst of constant pain and discomfort, this sudden manifestation of His tangible presence totally caught me off guard.

But as I lay there feeling the heavy blanket of His presence, He told me, "I'm rewarding your faith, Wanda!" I immediately felt the joy of His heart in my radical decision to trust Him in doing something as crazy as chewing nicotine gum! I felt at that moment that He could have directed me to do any number of things, but the focus wasn't the "what" but the "Who." All He wanted was for me to listen to His voice, trust Him, and follow His lead. He was demonstrating His delight and pleasure in my childlike faith to trust Him in the midst of pain, discouragement, and a totally radical treatment idea. Not only did I feel His close presence hovering over me, I could also sense angels nearby who were laughing at the enemy, rejoicing in my victory, and cheering me on in my walk of faith.

As a result of my simple obedience I was overcome by His presence, reassured of His love, and strengthened in my faith. Just the night before, I had been awakened, yet again, by a spirit of fear. Sensing that Holy Spirit was about to do something powerful, the enemy was trying to harass me and immobilize my faith. I had awoken with great trepidation and apprehension in trying this whole nicotine idea. But by joining in agreement with Bobby the following morning and stepping out in faith, that spirit of fear was immediately dealt with, and the joy of the Lord flooded my soul.

"And without faith it is impossible to please Him,
for whoever would draw near to God must believe that He exists and
that He rewards those who seek Him." (Hebrews 11:6)

Seeming Contradictions

Interestingly, I was surprised to realize that the ring in my ear was still there. Even as I was experiencing the powerful presence of the Lord, my ear was still ringing! So, even as I took in this powerful encounter, I instinctively knew this journey was far from over. This was not the culmination of my faith, nor was this the key to my healing. And as amazing as this sudden visitation was, it wasn't the high point of my journey. It was only the beginning.

That first dose was just the start of ongoing visitations and encounters with the Lord. The nicotine protocol called for me to chew nicotine gum four times a day. I had only taken the first dose that morning and had three more to go. Upon taking the second dose a few hours later, I was stunned when the same thing happened. Five minutes after chewing the gum, the Holy Spirit came upon me again in the same measure and I had to sit down to take it all in. Lasting almost an hour, His overwhelming presence was just as strong and just as surprising.

This continued with the third and fourth dose that day - and continued the next day, and the next - after every dose. The tangible and powerful presence of the Lord descended upon me each and every time I took a dose of this strange protocol. What became rather humorous was that instead of becoming addicted to nicotine, I was becoming addicted to His presence! And that's exactly what He wanted. He was teaching me how to recognize His tangible presence and to set aside whatever I was doing and simply yield. Because His weight was so strong, I had already known to sit down whenever I took a dose so I wouldn't keel over somewhere and hurt myself. It was apparent that He was taking me much deeper than anticipated and giving me keys to healing that I'd never considered. The reality was, even if my body wasn't being physically healed yet in the way I expected, my soul and spirit were being radically healed and transformed. His presence became my medicine. Literally!

In each of these encounters, He revealed something different about His character. He would show me His love, His tenderness, His power, and many other aspects of His nature. One Sunday afternoon, I was overwhelmed with His beauty. I had never felt impressed by this before, and my heart was overwhelmed when He poured over me a liquid love and revelation of how beautiful He was. I wept and rejoiced in this new revelation and actually told Him to stop as I didn't think my physical body could handle so much glory! The truth was - what had started as a nightmare a few months before was now turning into heavenly encounters I never could have imagined. I was finding HIM.

And yet, throughout the coming days of visitation – the ring continued. This divine contradiction forced me to learn things I didn't know I needed. Not only was I recognizing His presence and receiving increased wisdom and insight into heavenly realities, He was also strengthening my resolve and perseverance. He was building my character and putting something inside of me that I knew would be needed for future assignments and mandates.

"Not only that, but we rejoice in our sufferings, knowing that suffering produces endurance, and endurance produces character, and character produces hope, and hope does not put us to shame, because God's love has been poured into our hearts through the Holy Spirit who has been given to us." (Romans 5:3-5 ESV)

Throughout the days of visitation, I began to embrace the process instead of fighting it. I knew He was doing a sacred work and I couldn't rush the process. I also knew that the gift of resourcing that He had given me would be helpful for countless others who were struggling with physical attacks and chronic health issues.

Underlying Causes

As the Lord began to teach me about underlying root causes, He led me down a rabbit hole. I began to learn the truths about inflammation and the various toxins in our bodies that cause many of the symptoms both Bobby and I were experiencing. We learned how many of our food sources were laden with man-made products that were extremely unhealthy and damaging. Recognizing for the first time that my constant nasal congestion and seasonal stuffiness was not normal, and should be treated, I went off all gluten, dairy, seed oils, and processed foods. I had never considered that inflammation in my sinuses could produce an irritating ring! I began to actually listen to my body and pay attention to what I was eating and how it affected me. The scripture about "rightly discerning the body" took on a whole new meaning for me (1 Corinthians 11:29)!

I also learned about many of the natural supplements and healing remedies that God had already put within nature to treat and cure our ailments. I started using castor oil packs to help loosen up and drain my lymphatic system and began to find relief. I could tell the difference when cutting out certain foods and taking the right vitamins. We were finally beginning to understand health from a wholistic perspective, not dependent on man-made drugs or manufactured medicines. We both went on a heavy-metal detox, and I did a parasite cleanse. We began to be more mindful about what vitamins and minerals we each needed and became intentional in formulating a plan for long-term health. As a result, little by little, the sound in my ear began to decrease even more. Bobby began to feel a return of energy as we began to exercise together, and we knew we were on the right track. As we heeded every directive the Lord gave us and prayed together consistently, we saw gradual improvement both physically and spiritually.

The Biggest Revelation

In the midst of all the revelation the Lord was giving about healing protocols, I was determined to make my faith in Him the priority. Even with all the practical wisdom He was giving us, we sensed it would still take some supernatural intervention to overcome some of the lingering issues we faced. I've always known the power of declaring His Word and wondered if I didn't need to do more of this on a daily basis. One morning when I was thinking about this, the Lord interrupted my thought process to bring me the revelation I needed to hear:

"This is more about getting to know Me as your Healer than it is in getting your healing."

The truth of His tender rebuke freed me from condemnation, but also challenged me. How much of my faith for healing was focused on getting my breakthrough instead of getting to know Him as Healer? How much was I bypassing conversation with Him just to recite more scriptures or collect more information about my symptoms? It was a reminder that this wasn't about seeking a word for healing, but seeking His heart. This is where our faith must rest. Not just in what He says – but in who He is. It's our confidence in His unconditional love and care for us that will determine the true level of our faith. It's our absolute belief in His goodness that must be the core of our faith. Even in the midst of contradictions and disappointments, we must believe that He is altogether good and wants us healed and set free.

Baptism by Fire

I was now six months into this journey, and I still had no idea where He was taking me. I had been doing the nicotine protocol for several weeks and was still reveling in His ongoing presence. I eventually realized that the remaining ring in my ear was not caused by anything related to Covid as the nicotine had little physical impact. Even so, it was clear that the Lord used the nicotine protocol as a touch point for my faith and a means to bring me into His presence on a consistent basis. Because of the research I had done, I was now able to suggest this possible remedy for others. Even though the nicotine didn't make any visible difference, my physical symptoms were still slowly improving.

I continued to follow every directive the Lord gave me, and I was constantly reminded of His oversight in this journey. I continued to stand on His Word and yield to His presence. Still, I was desperate to be free of the (level 3) ring and had yet to experience the big breakthrough I was hoping for. And then, the Lord surprised me yet again.

One night around 3 a.m. I was stirred awake. I sensed Him kneeling down right beside me at my bed and He immediately whispered in my ear, "It's Me. I'm here." He wanted to assure me of this, because only a few moments later I began to feel my entire body on fire. It came on so suddenly I was initially frightened. It felt like I was being electrocuted. From the top of my head to the bottom of my toes, I felt my body react to something I'd never experienced before.

My first reaction was fear. I actually began to wonder if the nicotine was beginning to have a negative affect on my body and I woke up Bobby. He saw my distress and quickly assessed my condition to make sure I was OK. But even as he was asking me questions and checking my temperature, I suddenly remembered the words: "It's Me. I'm here." It was then that I realized I was not experiencing some negative physical reaction to the nicotine, but experiencing a powerful download of the supernatural kind.

"I baptize you with water for repentance, but He who is coming after me is mightier than I, whose sandals I am not worthy to carry. He will baptize you with the Holy Spirit and fire." (Matthew 3:11 ESV)

I had heard others speak of a "baptism of fire," but had no clue what that was or how it might feel. Yet, I knew that my body was on fire – and that it was totally of the Lord. Instead of feeling the usual warm blanket of His presence, or even the tingling and shaking of His Spirit that I had known many times before, this sensation was on another level. It felt like I was being "plugged in" to something and getting electrically charged! As I lay there, unable to move, I knew I could only yield. Whatever He was doing, I couldn't escape it. Nor did I want to. It was terrifying – yet glorious. I knew I was touching something outside this realm, and it was touching me. There was no doubt whatsoever that I was being radically touched from above. The fire of the Lord continued to burn for over an hour and gradually subsided after two. Even as I woke up the next morning, I could still feel the lingering affects of the encounter.

"Then one of the seraphim flew to me, having in his hand a burning coal that he had taken with tongs from the altar. And he touched my mouth and said: "Behold, this has touched your lips; your guilt is taken away, and your sin atoned for." (Isaiah 6:6-7)

I immediately went to Scriptures and began to inquire of the Lord. What was this and what was it for!? Why now!? The Holy Spirit took me to Isaiah 6 where the prophet came to the mercy seat of God and encountered His presence. Feeling totally unqualified to be a spokesman for the Lord, Isaiah was undone in the midst of God's glory. But it was there at the Throne of God that the seraphim, "the burning one," came with a coal of fire and placed it on Isaiah's lips. Upon receiving this fire from the altar, the prophet was totally transformed. No longer hanging his head in shame, he quickly responded to the Lord's invitation and said, "Here I am. Send me!" The fire of God had burned up his fleshly weakness and fear, and radically emboldened him with a zeal of the Lord to fulfill his call.

Upon learning more of this baptism of fire, I was both humbled and in awe. After all that I had gone through, to experience this was beyond anything I could have imagined. In the midst of the worst pain and struggle of my life, here I was experiencing these other-worldly realities that showcased God's love, power, and supernatural presence. My attempts at "getting my healing" were now being overshadowed and overwhelmed by getting to know Him. He was going far beyond just healing my body. He was transforming me – mind, will, and emotions – from the inside out. He was inviting me even deeper into a work of the Spirit that I had never known before.

I would experience this same "burning" for the next two nights. Each time, I was awakened to find my entire body on fire. I would simply yield to the presence of the Lord and listen. I knew I was getting a transfusion, and I desperately needed it. I didn't know where it would lead, but I was determined to let Him do His work. Whether it would eventually lead to full physical healing, or more valleys and tests, I didn't know. But by this time, it didn't matter. I was touching Him in ways I never felt worthy of. The heartaches, suffering, and unanswered questions from this journey were now very small compared to the glories I was experiencing.

"For I consider that the sufferings of this present time are not worth comparing with the glory that is to be revealed to us."
(Romans 8:18 ESV)

As I sought the Lord concerning the many encounters in this journey, I was continually humbled. Even though I questioned His methods, His timing, and how He could "allow" some of the suffering I experienced, He was showing Himself to be a perfect Father. He loved me enough to challenge me and bring out the best in me (Hebrews 12:7-11). The apostle Paul exhorted believers to "share in the fellowship of His sufferings" (Philippians 3:10). Though Jesus never suffered due to physical illness, He was familiar with grief, disappointment, and pain. He demonstrated that our earthly pain doesn't have to end in despair or defeat. When yielded to Him, it can become a tool that brings victory over the flesh and the devil, and a greater manifestation of His Kingdom power and authority.

There isn't any guarantee of a trouble-free life when surrendering to the Lord. There's only the absolute promise that He will be with us throughout the struggles and the setbacks. Some of the deepest revelations and most profound truths can only be found in the desert. But just as Jesus came out of His wilderness of testing with increased authority and anointing, so can we!

From Glory to Glory

In the months that followed, Bobby and I continued to yield to His direction and implement many of the things He was teaching us – both spiritually and practically. And though the fire of His presence gradually waned in subsequent months, it continues to simmer deep within my being. At the writing of this book, my tinnitus is virtually gone and we continue to see improvement in Bobby's eyes. We have continued to learn about the natural helps that are available for our physical well-being and are learning what it means to live in divine health instead of just looking for divine healing. What we thought we knew about healing has been radically altered. We believe God desires for us to be whole, not just healed.

"Now may the God of peace Himself sanctify you completely,
and may your whole spirit and soul and body be kept blameless
at the coming of our Lord Jesus Christ. He who calls you is faithful;
He will surely do it." (1 Thessalonians 5:23-24)

What I learned throughout this journey has changed my life. The Lord took me through some valleys of despair in order to bring me to some mountaintops of glory. The revelations I received about His ways, His means, and His methods have forever changed me. Physical healing is one thing - spiritual health and vitality are another. And if I had to choose between the two, I'd rather have pain with the Glory instead of healing with no Presence. Yet, we don't have to choose! He offers us the full package of healing, restoration, AND glory – if we but yield to the process. How that looks will be different for everyone.

When people ask us to pray for their healing, we now look beyond just the presenting symptoms and ask for the wisdom of God in order to assess rightly. Many of the physical symptoms we experience are caused by something else. Medically speaking, the goal should always be to find the root cause and not just give medications to ease the visible symptoms. The same is true spiritually. Our bodies can often reflect that which is happening in our thoughts and emotions. Any toxic mindsets or unhealed areas of our soul can wreak havoc on our bodies. This is why we must make our sensitivity to His voice such a priority and seek His heart even more than a physical touch. He knows what actually needs healing first and will guide us through to complete restoration and wholeness.

"May the God of endurance and encouragement grant you to live in such harmony with one another, in accord with Christ Jesus, that together you may with one voice glorify the God and Father of our Lord Jesus Christ."
(Romans 15:5-6)

We also believe that faith is best activated when there is a complete alignment with the Father's heart, as well as with those we pray with. Just as Bobby and I saw the increased power and authority of our unified prayers, so believers must learn the power of our oneness of spirit to nullify and immobilize principalities and powers. As we agree from the heart, and not just our mouths, we will see the enemy's strongholds broken and healing will be released to the Body like never before. I believe there are regional spirits of infirmity in place that are greatly limiting our prayers for healing. It will take a corporate agreement to break these strongholds and see a flood of healing be released to the Body of Christ. (I write more about this at the end of the book.)

In sharing my own journey, I hope you are encouraged to see the beauty of the process. Obviously, what I experienced is unique to me. I'm certainly not suggesting that everything I experienced will happen to anyone else who follows a similar path. Your journey is specially tailored for you. God knows what He's already put inside of you, and He wants you to discover the power of the resurrected Christ within! Regardless of the challenges you face, He will walk with you every step of the way and teach you what to do, and how to do it. Do not let any suffering or pain deter you. Physical symptoms do not determine the outcome! They are only temporary side effects of our fallen state. His grace is greater, and He will use it all for your good and His glory. Just don't quit, and don't stop believing. Your pursuit of Him will bring a reward far greater than you ever imagined and will be totally worth the cost of the journey.

Words for Healing

He is Always Faithful

Numbers 23:19
God is not human, that He should lie, not a human being, that He should change His mind. Does He speak and then not act? Does He promise and not fulfill?

Thank You, Lord, for keeping Your word in healing all our sicknesses and diseases. This is what You provided at the cross and it never expires. You haven't changed Your mind, and You never cancel a promise. I stand in the assurance of Your faithfulness to Your word and Your unchanging determination to make me whole.

Deuteronomy 31:6
Be strong and courageous. Do not be afraid or terrified because of them, for the Lord your God goes with you; He will never leave you nor forsake you.

Lord, thank You for not leaving me in my weakened state or giving up on me! Thank You for going before me and paving this path to health and well being. I am strong and courageous because the power of Your Spirit lives within me. I do not fear the unknown for You have already gone before and made a way through.

Deuteronomy 32:4
He is the Rock, His works are perfect, and all His ways are just. A faithful God who does no wrong, upright and just is He.

You are my Rock, O God! Your ways are perfect and the way You are leading me in this healing journey is just and good. You can do no wrong and are committed to my welfare and wholeness. Help me keep in step with You and stay faithful to Your directives.

1 Kings 8:56
Praise be to the Lord, who has given rest to His people Israel just as He promised. Not one word has failed of all the good promises He gave through His servant Moses.

Throughout history, You have been faithful to Your people, God. I can rest on this promise that not one Word of Yours will fail me. Remind me of these words so that I can find peace and not be troubled. Give me fresh words of hope so that I can stand firm in Your will to fully heal and restore.

Psalms 33:4
For the word of the Lord is right and true; He is faithful in all He does.

Father, You do not provide for healing at the cross and then not come through in victory. Everything You do is out of love for me and for my good. You can only do what is right and true. You are doing that now for me and I choose to trust You all the way through to completion of this process.

Psalms 40:11
Do not withhold Your mercy from me, Lord; may Your love and faithfulness always protect me.

Your love and faithfulness are like a shield about me, God. You cannot help but be faithful because of Your immense love that never fails. Even as I wait for the full manifestation of my healing, I know You are with me and are protecting me from evil.

Psalms 89:33-34
But I will not take My love from him, nor will I ever betray My faithfulness. I will not violate My covenant or alter what My lips have uttered.

Lord, You have committed Yourself to be faithful. You will not change Your promise to heal, nor will You alter what You have already provided through the cross. You are proving Your faithfulness even more than mine! Thank You for being so determined to see me healed so that Your Word will be upheld and Your name will be praised.

Jeremiah 17:14
Heal me, Lord, and I will be healed; save me and I will be saved, for You are the one I praise.

Father, You are the One that I look to for my needs and provision. You alone are worthy of praise for being a God who heals and restores all who call on Your name. You save all the afflicted because You are faithful and true. Thank You for being my Savior!

Matthew 24:35
Heaven and earth will pass away, but My words will never pass away.

Even when my condition seems to worsen and my pain is on the rise, You stay true to Your Word! You promise to bring me through to victory. I will not change my mind simply because of setbacks or seeming failures. I trust in Your Word alone to heal me because Your Word never fails.

John 16:33
I have told you these things, so that in Me you may have peace. In this world you will have trouble. But take heart! I have overcome the world.

Even in the midst of hardship and pain, Your peace is available to me. I lay aside my worries and anxieties and the fear of the unknown because You call me an overcomer! I choose to follow my Prince of Peace on this journey. I will not allow the enemy to rob me of my faith or my confidence in my Healer. The power of Christ has set me free from sickness and disease, and His power within me has already won the battle!

1 Corinthians 10:13
No temptation has overtaken you except what is common to mankind. And God is faithful; He will not let you be tempted beyond what you can bear. But when you are tempted, He will also provide a way out so that you can endure it.

I know You are with me in this healing journey, Lord. You know what I can handle, and what I can't. Thank You for using this experience to help me see the power of the risen Christ that is already within me. Thank You for challenging me in my faith and showing me what is truly possible. I trust You to guard my steps. I know You will never let me down or let me fall.

Philippians 1:6
Being confident of this, that He who began a good work in you will carry it on to completion until the day of Christ Jesus.

Lord, You never start something and then leave it unfinished. You have started a healing work in my life, and You aim to complete it in victory. Thank You for walking me through this journey of faith. I remain confident and steadfast in Your unfailing love and Your faithfulness in taking me through to the finish.

2 Thessalonians 3:3
But the Lord is faithful, and He will strengthen you and protect you from the evil one.

Lord, You are faithful in strengthening me and protecting me from the enemy. Even as I contend for my healing, You put boundaries around me that keep the enemy at bay and unable to harass me. Thank You for watching over my life and being My Shield and Defender.

2 Timothy 2:13
If we are faithless, He remains faithful, for He cannot disown Himself.

Even when I waver in my faith and am not sure of my future, You do not change Your mind, Lord. You have already determined that You want me whole and walking in divine health. Thank You for not giving up on me even when I give up on myself. Thank You for staying true to Your Word, even when mine fails.

Hebrews 10:23
Let us hold unswervingly to the hope we profess, for He who promised is faithful.

Because of Your unchanging character, I refuse to change my confession of faith. You have already secured my healing and are always faithful to fulfill Your promise. You are my Healer, and I agree with Your Word and not my symptoms, my setbacks, or any current weakness!

Hebrews 11:11
And by faith even Sarah, who was past childbearing age, was enabled to bear children because she considered Him faithful who had made the promise.

It's never too late to be healed! Regardless of how much time has passed or how impossible it seems, You are always faithful to fulfill Your promise! Thank You for keeping Your word and not being bound by time. You are bound to Your Word and I fully trust in You to complete my healing!

James 1:17
Every good and perfect gift is from above, coming down from the Father of the heavenly lights, who does not change like shifting shadows.

Lord, I confess that my faith can change from day to day depending on my feelings, my symptoms, and my surroundings. But You, O Lord, never change! You are faithful in all You do and never waiver in Your determination to see me victorious and fully healed. Thank You for staying true, even when I falter.

NOTES

His Compassions Never Fail

Nehemiah 9:17
They refused to listen and failed to remember the miracles You performed among them. They became stiff-necked and in their rebellion appointed a leader in order to return to their slavery. But You are a forgiving God, gracious and compassionate, slow to anger and abounding in love. Therefore, You did not desert them.

It's amazing that You continue to love me and show me compassion when I fail to listen or give up on Your promise! Because of Your compassion, You do not turn Your back on me or give up on seeing this through. Thank You for not leaving me in my current state of bondage. You are determined to see me whole and free!

Jeremiah 30:17
"But I will restore you to health and heal your wounds," declares the Lord, "because you are called an outcast, Zion for whom no one cares."

It is because of Your great love and mercy that You reach down to heal Your people. You see when the enemy overwhelms us. Your compassion compels You to respond to our cries for help. Thank You for restoring my health and healing my wounds. Your compassions never fail!

Isaiah 49:15-16
"Can a mother forget the baby at her breast and have no compassion on the child she has borne?" Though she may forget, I will not forget you! See, I have engraved you on the palms of My hands; your walls are ever before Me.

Thank You, Lord, for being a loving Father who holds me close to Your heart. You created me and knew me before I was even conceived. You knew I would have need of healing before I did. You hold me close in Your hands and surround me with care. Even if others forget about me, You never will.

Isaiah 54:10

"Though the mountains be shaken and the hills be removed, yet My unfailing love for you will not be shaken nor My covenant of peace be removed," says the Lord, who has compassion on you.

Even when my condition worsens and circumstances seem darker, Your love is constant and Your peace ever present. You promise to hold me up and keep me in the palm of Your hand. I receive Your peace in the midst of the storm, knowing that Your compassion compels You to bring me healing and wholeness. Help me keep my mind fixed on this truth as I trust in You.

Psalms 6:8-10

Away from me, all you who do evil, for the Lord has heard my weeping. The Lord has heard my cry for mercy; the Lord accepts my prayer. All my enemies will be overwhelmed with shame and anguish; they will turn back and suddenly be put to shame.

You hear my cries for help, God, and accept my prayers because of Your great mercy. You know the pain I have suffered and the conditions I face, and yet You promise to intervene on my behalf and overwhelm my enemies and any attack that has come against me. I do not have to fear what the enemy tries for Your presence is so much greater! You overcome every foe and scheme set against my health and well being. Thank You for hearing my cry.

Psalms 103:13

As a father has compassion on his children, so the Lord has compassion on those who fear Him.

You are not a heartless god who does not care about my condition or weakened state. You are a loving Father who cares deeply about me. I know You have been looking out for me and have been watching over this entire journey. I trust You completely as a Good Father who will continue to carry me through and hold my heart in the palm of Your hands.

Psalms 145:8-9
The Lord is gracious and compassionate, slow to anger and rich in love. The Lord is good to all; He has compassion on all He has made.

Thank You for reminding me that You are slow to anger and rich in love. Forgive me for thinking You have run out of patience with me or are frustrated with my slowness in learning. You are a gracious Father who delights in simply walking with me through this entire healing process.

Micah 7:19
You will again have compassion on us; You will tread our sins underfoot and hurl all our iniquities into the depths of the sea.

Even when I miss the mark and make a mistake, Your compassion and mercy prevails! When I turn to You and heed Your voice, You love to answer my cries for help. You took my sins as well as sicknesses on the cross and have determined their end. Thank You for Your passionate love for me that is determined to see me walk in victory!

Matthew 9:36
When He saw the crowds, He had compassion on them, because they were harassed and helpless, like sheep without a shepherd.

Lord, Your heart is drawn to those who are harassed by the devil and those who feel helpless against attacks. Thank You for being my Good Shepherd and empathizing with my pain. Thank You for having compassion on my condition and coming to my aid. Thank You for responding to my cries for help and loving me so fully and completely.

Matthew 14:14
When Jesus landed and saw a large crowd, He had compassion on them and healed their sick.

It is Your compassion, Lord, that leads You to heal us and make us whole. Thank You for caring for Your people and understanding our plight. Forgive me when I start to think You don't really care. Remind me of how big Your heart is and how much You truly feel for me.

Mark 8:2-3
I have compassion for these people; they have already been with Me three days and have nothing to eat. If I send them home hungry, they will collapse on the way, because some of them have come a long distance.

Not only is Your love and compassion ever present, You see my every need. You see my comings and goings and know what I will face. You have already planned ahead for me because You care so deeply about my life. Thank You for providing everything I need in order to be healed, whole, and completely free, in Jesus' name!

Luke 7:13
When the Lord saw her, His heart went out to her and He said, "Don't cry."

Thank You, Lord, for feeling my pain and understanding my condition. Thank You for reaching out to me and comforting me in my distress. I receive Your words of comfort and desire to see the end result as You do. You cheer me up and encourage me to fix my eyes on my healing to come!

NOTES

NOTES

He Heals Our Spirit

Proverbs 15:13
A happy heart makes the face cheerful, but heartache crushes the spirit.

Lord, watch over my spirit that I not give in to heart ache or despair. Bring me Your Word that will lift my heart and bring joy to my soul, mind, and body. I choose a cheerful heart instead of crushing pain.

Isaiah 11:2
And the Spirit of the Lord shall rest upon him, the Spirit of wisdom and understanding, the Spirit of counsel and might, the Spirit of knowledge and the fear of the Lord.

Lord, I receive the fullness of Your Holy Spirit so that I can discern rightly, judge accurately, and walk forward in absolute confidence of Your goodness and providential care. Thank you for resting on me, Holy Spirit, and giving me everything I need to succeed and walk in the fullness of life. Thank You for teaching me everything I need to know in order to be whole.

Zechariah 4:6
So he said to me, "This is the word of the Lord to Zerubbabel: Not by might, nor by power, but by My Spirit, says the Lord Almighty.

It is by Your Spirit, Lord, that I am healed. It is not by my mighty efforts or even my will to change, but a supernatural work of Your Spirit which gives me faith, hope, and all that is needed for healing to manifest. May my spirit be fully immersed in Your presence and transformed by Your love, and I will give You all the glory for the breakthroughs to come!

John 6:63
The Spirit gives life; the flesh counts for nothing. The words I have spoken to you - they are full of the Spirit and life.

Remind me of Your words, Lord, and recount Your promises and intentions. Forgive me for yielding to my own thoughts and ways and forgetting where true life comes from. Help me put away my own imaginations and ideas and replace them with Your words that alone bring hope, joy, and fullness of life. Remind me of what You have said so that I will remain steadfast in faith.

John 7:38-39a

"Whoever believes in Me, as Scripture has said, rivers of living water will flow from within them." By this He meant the Spirit, whom those who believed in Him were later to receive.

Father, fill my spirit with rivers of Your living water. I want to drink from Your Spirit so that I will never be thirsty again. Refresh my soul and rejuvenate my whole being with a fresh baptism of Your Spirit to overflowing. Wash away all doubt and fear so that I can walk in pure faith for Your healing grace upon my life.

Romans 8:15

The Spirit you received does not make you slaves, so that you live in fear again; rather, the Spirit you received brought about your adoption to sonship. And by Him we cry, "Abba, Father."

Father, I am Your child! I am no longer a slave to fear or doubt because You purchased me as Your own. Thank You for adopting me as your son/daughter and giving me access to all Your promises, including healing of my soul, spirit, mind, and body. You are a good Father, and I thank You now for Your perfect love which heals completely and sets me free!

1 Corinthians 2:12

What we have received is not the spirit of the world, but the Spirit who is from God, so that we may understand what God has freely given us.

Lord, I will not listen to the world or those who do not know You for the understanding of my plight. Remind me of what You have already freely given at the cross and purchased with Your blood. Though it doesn't make sense in the natural, I thank you for the gift of the Spirit by which I can know Your will, walk in Your ways, and stand fast in faith for Your healing to manifest in my life.

1 Corinthians 6:19
Do you not know that your bodies are temples of the Holy Spirit, who is in you, whom you have received from God? You are not your own.

My body is Your temple, Holy Spirit! That means that You intend to dwell in a holy place that is free from sickness, disease, and torment! This body is not my own, but Yours! Teach me how to take care of it. Thank You for watching over this House and cleansing it from sickness and sanctifying it by Your Spirit. May my body reflect the fullness of healing that only heaven can bring.

Galatians 5:16-17
So I say, walk by the Spirit, and you will not gratify the desires of the flesh. For the flesh desires what is contrary to the Spirit, and the Spirit what is contrary to the flesh. They are in conflict with each other so that you are not to do whatever you want.

Lord, forgive me when I keep trying to figure things out myself and walk in the flesh. Teach me to discern rightly between what feels good or seems right, and that which is truly of Your Spirit and will work. Cleanse my thoughts and intentions so that I will think like You and choose Your ways over my own. I trust You to know what is best for me and to establish all of my steps in this healing journey.

Galatians 5:25
Since we live by the Spirit, let us keep in step with the Spirit.

Establish every one of my steps, Lord. Alert me when I go astray and forget to ask for Your directions. Teach me to easily recognize when it is Your Spirit that is speaking and leading the way versus when I stray away and lean into my own thoughts and understanding. You alone know my path to complete healing, and I choose to listen to Your voice more than any other.

Ephesians 1:17-19
I keep asking that the God of our Lord Jesus Christ, the glorious Father, may give you the Spirit of wisdom and revelation, so that you may know Him better. I pray that the eyes of your heart may be enlightened in order

that you may know the hope to which He has called you, the riches of His glorious inheritance in His holy people, and His incomparably great power for us who believe.

Lord, give me the eyes of Your Spirit in order for me to see You more clearly. Fill me with the Spirit of wisdom and revelation so that I can see Your perfect plan concerning my healing. Reveal what needs to be seen so I can come into complete agreement with Your heart for me. Thank you for giving me a rich inheritance in this life and the power to know You more fully. I desire to get to know You as my Healer and not just focus on getting my healing. You are my glorious Father whose love is more than enough!

Ephesians 3:16-17a
I pray that out of His glorious riches He may strengthen you with power through His Spirit in your inner being, so that Christ may dwell in your hearts through faith.

Strengthen me, Lord, to be filled with Your faith for my healing. Where I am weak, fill me with the power of Your Spirit to rightly believe and place my hope in Your unfailing love.

2 Timothy 1:7 (ESV)
For God gave us a spirit not of fear but of power and love and self-control.

Father, I will not submit myself to a spirit of fear but receive the power of Your love through Your Spirit. Fill me with a greater measure of Your love to overcome any fears or doubts about Your working in my life. Help me to control my anxious thoughts by replacing them with the truths of Your Spirit which always bring life and hope.

NOTES

NOTES

He Heals Our Soul

Psalms 73:26
My flesh and my heart may fail, but God is the strength of my heart and my portion forever.

Though I feel weak at times and my faith fails, You are always my anchor and my source of strength. I will not try and determine what is true based on my physical weaknesses or shortcomings, but rather choose to place my hope and faith in who You are – always faithful and always Perfect Love.

Psalms 103:2-5
Praise the Lord, my soul, and forget not all His benefits - who forgives all your sins and heals all your diseases, who redeems your life from the pit and crowns you with love and compassion, who satisfies your desires with good things so that your youth is renewed like the eagle's.

I praise You Jesus, for healing all our sicknesses and diseases through Your sacrifice on the cross. You paid for them ALL! Your desire is to heal me, restore me, and renew me back to life. I don't have to do anything more to earn this benefit – You willingly died so that I might be healed and whole. This is the truth I embrace and the hope I will cling to as I wait for my body to catch up to what You've already done!

Proverbs 12:25
Anxiety weighs down the heart, but a kind word cheers it up.

Lord, I do not want anxiety or worrisome thoughts to weigh down my soul. Bring me words that will cheer my heart and lighten my load. Thank You for Your Word which always brings hope and a bright future. Bring into the light any thought that is causing my soul to be weighed down so that I can receive healing through Your words of cheer and kindness.

Proverbs 17:22
A cheerful heart is good medicine, but a crushed spirit dries up the bones.

Forgive me, Lord, for allowing disappointments and discouragement to wreak havoc on my body. I lay these strongholds down and ask You to replace them with the good news of Your steadfast love and determination to heal me. Help me to laugh at the enemy and to find joy in the simple pleasures of life. Bring me the medicine of gladness to displace a spirit of heaviness so that my body can be healed.

Luke 1:46
And Mary said, "My soul magnifies the Lord, and my spirit rejoices in God my Savior.

Just as Mary did, so will I magnify the Lord in all things. I speak to my spirit and say, "Rejoice in the Lord!" I choose to magnify my Lord for this journey knowing that He is using all of it to bring Him greater glory and greater blessing to me. I don't have to understand it all – I merely rejoice in the fact that He has chosen me to pour Himself through so that others can know His love and goodness.

John 16:33
I have told you these things so that in Me you may have peace. In the world you will have trouble. But take heart; I have overcome the world.

Lord, You said we would experience trouble, yet we can have peace in the midst. Because of what You overcame on the cross, I too can overcome this temporary hardship and pain! I receive Your peace to sustain me on this healing journey knowing that You are leading me to full restoration and abundant life ahead!

Romans 15:13
May the God of hope fill you with all joy and peace as you trust in Him so that you may overflow with hope by the power of the Holy Spirit.

Fill me, Lord, with Your joy and peace. Give me reason to hope. Divert my thoughts and attention from those things that only cause me anxiety and fear. Point me to Your truth that is filled with good things in my fu-

ture. Remind me when my soul becomes weary so that I can redirect my thoughts towards You.

2 Corinthians 9:8
And God is able to bless you abundantly, so that in all things at all times, having all that you need, you will abound in every good work.

I will not be limited by my own resources, but trust in You, Lord, to give me everything I need to succeed. Even as I contend for Your healing grace to fully manifest, I believe You want to bless me in abundant ways. Help me see where You are providing for me and pouring out Your goodness in other areas of my life so that I can give You thanks and praise.

2 Corinthians 12:9
But He said to me, "My grace is sufficient for you, for My power is made perfect in weakness." Therefore, I will boast all the more gladly about my weaknesses, so that Christ's power may rest on me.

You delight to show Yourself strong, Lord. Even in my weakest state, You come and flow through me and work through me in amazing ways. It's when I'm at my lowest point that Your love and compassion rush towards me to show Yourself strong on my behalf. Thank You for revealing Your power through me when I have nothing left of my own. Your grace is amazing!

Philippians 4:6-7
Do not be anxious about anything, but in every situation, by prayer and petition, with thanksgiving, present your requests to God. And the peace of God, which transcends all understanding, will guard your hearts and your minds in Christ Jesus.

I will not be anxious about my present condition! I will not let my fears and doubts take residence in my heart but will pour out my troubles to You and lay them at Your feet. Thank You for listening and trading my sorrows for Your peace and presence. Thank You for coming and standing guard over my heart and mind so that I can stay in a place of peace and rest. You alone can provide this reality. Thank You for filling my soul with all things good, true, and right.

Hebrews 9:14

How much more, then, will the blood of Christ, who through the eternal Spirit offered Himself unblemished to God, cleanse our consciences from acts that lead to death, so that we may serve the living God!

Remind me of the power of Your blood, Lord! It is through Your blood that my anxious thoughts and doubts can be washed clean. It is through Your blood that I have access to Your power to overcome sickness and death. I am not bound to my fleshly thoughts and ideas when I apply Your blood to my soul, mind, and body. You were the perfect sacrifice for me, and because of Your death and resurrection, I have all the power I need to be free, healed, and whole!

James 1:2-4

Consider it pure joy, my brothers and sisters, whenever you face trials of many kinds, because you know that the testing of your faith produces perseverance. Let perseverance finish its work so that you may be mature and complete, not lacking anything.

I choose to face this present trial with joy! Lord, You told us that we would face trials and hardships, but only because of what You are accomplishing through them – for our good. I trust You with this process and rejoice in Your ultimate plans for my life. You have asked me to persevere and to be steadfast in my faith because it will produce an outcome that will give You all the glory and be a great blessing to me. Everything You do is for good - and for that – I rejoice!

James 4:7

Submit yourselves, then, to God. Resist the devil, and he will flee from you.

I speak to my soul and say, "Submit to the Lord!" Do not let the devil have his way in filling you with dread and despair! Resist the enemy of your soul and cling to the Lord who stands by and champions your victory. Thank You, Lord, for Your overwhelming presence that causes every demon to tremble and every enemy to instantly leave!

1 Peter 5:7

Casting all your anxiety on Him because He cares for you.

If I have ever doubted Your care and concern for me, Lord, forgive me. You have already proven Your overwhelming love for me by what You did on the cross to secure my freedom and healing. I not only yield my anxious thoughts to you, but throw them at your feet, refusing them access to my soul! I will not allow any thoughts of harm or defeat to take hold of my soul but cast them all on You. You already overcame them all. Thank You for Your immense compassion for all that I am walking through and Your willingness to walk with me every step of the way.

3 John 1:2

Dear friend, I pray that you may enjoy good health and that all may go well with you, even as your soul is getting along well.

Lord, help me to keep my soul healthy and in a good place. My body often reflects what is going on in my mind and soul, so alert me when my thoughts become heavy and toxic. Teach me how to steward my soul's health so that I live from a place of rest and peace instead of reacting to my body's weaknesses. You desire for me to be entirely whole. Thank You for guiding me through this process.

NOTES

He Heals Our Mind

Isaiah 26:3
You will keep in perfect peace those whose minds are steadfast because they trust in You.

Thank You for Your perfect peace that keeps my mind at ease and at rest. Help me to stay steadfast in guarding my thought life so that You will remain the Prince of Peace in how I think. Keep me focused on Your truth and remind me when I wander away from fully trusting You in my healing process. Your peace is perfect, and I desire to live from this reality as the source of my strength.

Lamentations 3:22-24
Because of the Lord's great love we are not consumed, for His compassions never fail. They are new every morning; great is Your faithfulness. I say to myself, "The Lord is my portion; therefore, I will wait for Him."

This healing journey is a daily walk, and I choose to start each day by voicing my absolute trust and confidence in You. Your compassion and mercy never lack, and Your faithfulness is constant. Others will let me down and circumstances will change, but Your goodness and desire to complete my healing never changes and is always full to overflowing. I receive all that You've done for me and continue to wait for the full unveiling of Your promises over my life and purpose.

John 14:27
Peace, I leave with you; My peace I give you. I do not give to you as the world gives. Do not let your hearts be troubled and do not be afraid.

I choose, now, to shake off the world's mindsets and ideas that are contrary to Your goodness, Lord. The world and the ways of the flesh will never give me the peace I need. Only You can give me a peace of soul and mind to sustain me in this healing journey. I will not give in to troubling thoughts or wayward paths, but cling to Your presence as the source of my peace and provision.

Romans 8:6
The mind governed by the flesh is death, but the mind governed by the Spirit is life and peace.

I invite You, Holy Spirit, to stand watch over my mind and help me govern my thoughts. Show me when my thinking is only producing doubt and fear instead of peace and rest. Remind me of Your words that are filled with life and hope. Alert me when the enemy tries to rob me of Your peace so I can evict him from my mind and look to You as the governor of my thoughts.

Romans 15:13
May the God of hope fill you with all joy and peace as you trust in Him, so that you may overflow with hope by the power of the Holy Spirit.

I choose hope, Lord! I choose joy and peace in this healing process! Thank You for providing this option each and every day as I purpose to trust You above all else. I don't need to feel hopeless or in despair if I draw from Your presence on a daily basis. I can't do this on my own. I receive the power of Your Spirit to believe, to hope, and to expect the very best in the days to come.

Romans 16:20
The God of peace will soon crush Satan under your feet. The grace of our Lord Jesus Christ be with you.

This is Your promise, Lord! To crush Satan underneath my feet, including all the sickness and disease he has brought upon my life. It is Your peace that does this! Your victory over pain and suffering is absolute and I receive Your grace to stand. Your peace has the power to defeat and overcome the enemy of my soul and give me the wholeness I need.

2 Corinthians 5:17
Therefore, if anyone is in Christ, the new creation has come: The old has gone, the new is here!

Thank You for giving me the chance to start afresh, Lord! Thank You for demolishing the strongholds in my mind that have lied to me about who You really are. I receive the mind of Christ with which to now think like YOU! Thank You for making me a new person from the inside out. Thank You for giving me Your thoughts, Your ideas, and Your truth that will shatter the lies of the enemy and my flesh, and empower me to walk right into my freedom and healing.

2 Corinthians 10:4-6

The weapons we fight with are not the weapons of the world. On the contrary, they have divine power to demolish strongholds. We demolish arguments and every pretension that sets itself up against the knowledge of God, and we take captive every thought to make it obedient to Christ. And we will be ready to punish every act of disobedience, once your obedience is complete.

Lord, show me any thought in my mind that is not Yours. Show me any half-truth or twisted lie that is filling my mind so that I can use Your Word to demolish those strongholds of the enemy. I will not allow any thought that is contrary to Your heart, character, or Word into my thinking or belief system. I will not dwell on any thought that suggests You do not want me healed or set free. I receive Your power to cast down every vain imagination and apprehend Your truth that alone heals me and makes me whole.

Galatians 5:1

It is for freedom that Christ has set us free. Stand firm, then, and do not let yourselves be burdened again by a yoke of slavery.

I am not a slave to sin or bound to lies of the enemy. I refuse to become enslaved to faulty thinking or any belief that suggests God's love is not strong enough to heal me. I stand firm on His Word that states He has already paid the price for my healing and His blood is the cure. I speak to my mind to stay focused on God's full provision of healing, for He is the Healer of all!

Philippians 4:8

Finally, brothers and sisters, whatever is true, whatever is noble, whatever is right, whatever is pure, whatever is lovely, whatever is admirable - if anything is excellent or praiseworthy - think about such things.

Lord, I determine to think good thoughts that bring peace, joy, truth, and all things good from above. Help me focus on Your healing grace and Your goodness that reveal the fullness of Your glory. I will focus my thoughts on

Your promises for my good and welfare. I will not entertain any thought that robs me of Your joy and Your intention to bring me through this trial to complete victory.

1 Peter 1:13
Therefore, with minds that are alert and fully sober, set your hope on the grace to be brought to you when Jesus Christ is revealed at His coming.

Reveal Yourself to me, Jesus, and let me know the fullness of Your grace. You are coming alongside me to heal me and restore me. I set my mind on this truth and look forward to greater revelation of how great You are and how immense Your love is for me.

NOTES

NOTES

He Heals Our Body

Isaiah 40:29-31

He gives strength to the weary and increases the power of the weak. Even youths grow tired and weary, and young men stumble and fall; but those who hope in the Lord will renew their strength. They will soar on wings like eagles; they will run and not grow weary; they will walk and not be faint.

I speak to my body and say, "Be strong in the Lord and hope in His Word! Receive His supernatural power to revive this flesh and renew your strength. For your strength does not lie in your physical state, but in the power of His Spirit!" Thank You, Lord, for increasing my strength as I trust in You. I look to the day when I will run and not grow weary and will walk without failing. Because of Your presence in my life, my body will be revived and made strong once again.

Psalms 41:1-3

Blessed are those who have regard for the weak; the Lord delivers them in times of trouble. The Lord protects and preserves them - they are counted among the blessed in the land - He does not give them over to the desire of their foes. The Lord sustains them on their sickbed and restores them from their bed of illness.

Your compassion, O Lord, has power to heal. It is Your regard for the weak and helpless that releases a healing grace and protection. You are passionate in seeing the weak made strong and the sick made well. Grant me more of Your heart so I can embrace this truth to bring healing to my own body. Help me to regard others in similar conditions and pray for them that they, too, will be made well. Your promise is to not only sustain us in this healing journey, but to raise us up and restore us to full health.

Psalms 103:2-3

Praise the Lord, my soul, and forget not all His benefits - who forgives all your sins and heals all your diseases.

Lord, You consistently say in Your Word that you heal ALL. You do not play favorites, nor do You only pick and choose who You will heal. Your Word declares that You heal all who seek You and look to You for breakthrough. You paid for my healing on the cross. Nothing was left out! I do not have to work for this, but simply receive Your incredible gift of healing grace upon my life.

Proverbs 3:7-8

Do not be wise in your own eyes; fear the Lord and shun evil. This will bring health to your body and nourishment to your bones.

Forgive me, Lord, when I have looked to my own reasoning and resources instead of You for my healing. Forgive me for thinking I know better than You. Turn me away from ideas and thoughts that are coming from the enemy and my own flesh, and help me tune in to Your presence as my priority.

Jeremiah 17:14

Heal me, Lord, and I will be healed; save me and I will be saved, for You are the one I praise.

You are my source and my ultimate solution, Lord! Only You can truly save me from the traps of sickness in both my mind and body. I choose to praise You, regardless of my symptoms and circumstances, for You alone are the One who can heal me, deliver me, and set me free.

John 7:38-39a

"Whoever believes in Me, as Scripture has said, rivers of living water will flow from within them." By this He meant the Spirit, whom those who believed in Him were later to receive.

Lord, fill me again with the power of Your Spirit so I might draw from the endless well of life and power. May the rivers of the Holy Spirit flow through my life to touch every part of my soul, spirit, mind, and body. May this water renew and refresh me and bring me health and well-being. Remind me to draw from this well on a daily basis so that I will never be thirsty again.

Romans 12:1

Therefore, I urge you, brothers and sisters, in view of God's mercy, to offer your bodies as a living sacrifice, holy and pleasing to God - this is your true and proper worship.

Even in my weakened condition, I will worship You as my Healer and Redeemer. I will not lessen my praise or hesitate to declare Your goodness just because I can't see the whole picture right now. I willingly praise You as a sacrifice of worship. Take this body and use it as You see fit – for Your glory and Your praise. Sanctify me and make me a vessel that is holy and pleasing to You.

1 Corinthians 3:16

Don't you know that you yourselves are God's temple and that God's Spirit dwells in your midst.

This body is not my own but is the temple of Your Holy Spirit. Teach me to care for Your temple and to protect it and guard it from my own flesh and from the enemy's devices. Show me what changes I need to make so that my body has the best chance possible to thrive and be well. May my physical health be a reflection of who You are in all Your love and goodness.

1 Corinthians 6:12

"I have the right to do anything," you say - but not everything is beneficial. "I have the right to do anything" - but I will not be mastered by anything.

Holy Spirit, teach me how to properly steward my health. Show me what is good for my body and help me to know how to care for it properly. Forgive me for bad habits and strongholds of the flesh that have only made me weak and sick. Help me to choose rightly and to discipline my body so that I can be healthy and whole as You intend.

1 Corinthians 9:27 (ESV)

But I discipline my body and keep it under control, lest after preaching to others I myself should be disqualified.

Forgive me, Lord, for not always controlling my flesh and doing things that have only made my condition worse. Free me from strongholds of the flesh that I have become enslaved to. Help me to make good choices every day so I can develop good habits and a lifestyle that honors You.

2 Corinthians 4:16-17

Therefore we do not lose heart. Though outwardly we are wasting away, yet inwardly we are being renewed day by day. For our light and momentary troubles are achieving for us an eternal glory that far outweighs them all.

Thank You for reminding me that this body is only temporary, Lord! It does have its limits in the natural, but it does not have to limit Your wonder-working power in my life. Thank You for the life of Your Spirit that refreshes this decaying body and renews my strength. Thank You for working in my life so that I will gain an eternal reward for trusting in Your goodness and might.

Ephesians 5:29

After all, no one ever hated their own body, but they feed and care for their body, just as Christ does the church - for we are members of His body.

Cleanse me, Lord, of any hatred of this body and the condition I have found myself in. Where I have been frustrated, teach me how to be thankful in all things and to trust You in bringing me out of the cycles of sickness and weariness. Give me greater grace to appreciate what You have given me and give me a fresh desire to walk out this healing journey with gladness and joy.

Philippians 1:20

I eagerly expect and hope that I will in no way be ashamed, but will have sufficient courage so that now as always Christ will be exalted in my body, whether by life or by death.

Father, I want to honor You in every step of this process. Help me to get rid of bad practices and embrace all that is good and helpful to reflect Your goodness and love. Thank You for releasing me from any guilt or shame I have harbored because of my weakened state. I desire for this entire process to be a testimony of Your power and Your presence in my life, which is always perfect and complete.

NOTES

NOTES

He is Our Champion

Exodus 15:6
Your right hand, Lord, was majestic in power. Your right hand, Lord, shattered the enemy.

You not only go after my enemies, Lord, but You shatter them! By Your mighty right hand, You come down on the schemes of the enemy aimed at weakening my condition and robbing me of my health. I declare Your power and goodness in going after these powers aligned against me. Thank You for setting me free from their oppression!

Numbers 10:9
When you go into battle in your own land against an enemy who is oppressing you, sound a blast on the trumpets. Then you will be remembered by the Lord your God and rescued from your enemies.

Lord, I am sounding an alarm and raising my voice concerning my spiritual adversary who is oppressing me with sickness and disease. He has come to claim my body as territory for his dirty work. I renounce his trespassing and declare that You are the Lord of this temple and the Governor of my body. Thank you for setting me free from this enemy that seeks to torment me. Thank you for rescuing me and bringing me peace and soundness of mind, soul, and body.

Deuteronomy 32:39
See now that I myself am He! There is no god besides Me. I put to death and I bring to life, I have wounded and I will heal, and no one can deliver out of My hand.

There is no other god like You who has absolute and sovereign authority over sickness, disease, and death. You alone determine death and life. You alone will deliver me from my sickbed and raise me up again. The enemy has no such authority over my life, and I rejoice in Your all-encompassing power and love!

2 Chronicles 20:15

He said: "Listen, King Jehoshaphat and all who live in Judah and Jerusalem! This is what the Lord says to you: 'Do not be afraid or discouraged because of this vast army. For the battle is not yours, but God's.'"

I refuse to give in to fear or discouragement because I am not fighting this battle alone! Lord, You are standing in the gap for me and championing my complete healing and victory. I will not focus on the setbacks or disappointments but continue to trust in Your power to defeat this attack on my health. My symptoms do not dictate this journey, nor will bad days rob me of my trust in You. You are right here with me and are even more determined that I am to see healing and restoration manifest in my life.

2 Chronicles 20:17

You will not have to fight this battle. Take up your positions; stand firm and see the deliverance the Lord will give you, Judah and Jerusalem. Do not be afraid; do not be discouraged. Go out to face them tomorrow, and the Lord will be with you.

You have called me to stand firm in my faith, Lord. Regardless of the threats against my body, mind, and spirit, I will not give in to fear. Thank You for empowering me to stand up to the threats and say, "NO!" You have already defeated this enemy and paid for my healing. I do not have to do anything more, except to stand. Thank You for taking charge and going before me to demolish every attack and ambush set against me.

Job 8:21-22

He will yet fill your mouth with laughter and your lips with shouts of joy. Your enemies will be clothed in shame, and the tents of the wicked will be no more.

Thank You for the victory to come! Regardless of how the enemy has tried to attack me, I know the day is coming when my mouth will be filled with laughter and my lips will shout for joy. You will absolutely take out my enemies and that which has tried to destroy me shall be put to death by the power of Your blood!

Psalms 20:6-8

Now this I know: The Lord gives victory to His anointed. He answers him from His heavenly sanctuary with the victorious power of His right hand. Some trust in chariots and some in horses, but we trust in the name of the Lord our God. They are brought to their knees and fall, but we rise up and stand firm.

You are my Victorious Champion, Jesus, and you are cheering me on towards victory! You have heard my cry for healing and already answered me before I spoke. Your right hand is mighty in strength to defeat my enemies and overturn sickness and disease. It is Your name, O Lord, that has power to cripple the enemy and bring him to his knees. It is Your name that enables me to rise up and stand firm in faith. You are my Healer, and I rejoice in the power of Your name.

Psalms 33:16-19

No king is saved by the size of his army; no warrior escapes by his great strength. A horse is a vain hope for deliverance; despite all its great strength it cannot save. But the eyes of the Lord are on those who fear Him, on those whose hope is in His unfailing love, to deliver them from death and keep them alive in famine.

Though I will do my part in stewarding my health and taking care of this body, it is only You that can truly heal me and set me free, Jesus! No matter how many protocols I try or how many solutions I look for, I know that it is Your unfailing love that is the key to my healing. Help me to meditate on Your goodness and mercy, and Your desire to see me whole and complete. Fix my eyes on You so that my faith is fixed. I put my trust in Your never-failing love and compassion and not in my own efforts and strength.

Psalms 42:10-11

My bones suffer mortal agony as my foes taunt me, saying to me all day long, "Where is your God?" Why, my soul, are you downcast? Why so disturbed within me? Put your hope in God, for I will yet praise Him, my Savior and my God.

I refuse to listen to the enemy's taunts because of my physical condition! My God is not only with me, but He is for me and is my Healer and Redeemer! His love never fails, and I defy the voices that are trying to make me believe My God is not good. He is my salvation and my joy. My body's present condition does not determine His ultimate purpose to bring me out in wholeness and freedom.

Psalm 91:1-6

Whoever dwells in the shelter of the Most High will rest in the shadow of the Almighty. I will say of the Lord, "He is my refuge and my fortress, my God, in whom I trust." Surely He will save you from the fowler's snare and from the deadly pestilence. He will cover you with His feathers, and under His wings you will find refuge; His faithfulness will be your shield and rampart. You will not fear the terror of night, nor the arrow that flies by day, nor the pestilence that stalks in the darkness, nor the plague that destroys at midday.

Your presence is amazing, Lord! As I hide myself in You and daily seek Your face, You promise to protect me and guard me from all the snares and traps of the enemy. Not only will You defend me from spiritual invaders, but You grant me an increased level of faith to stand without fear. I do not have to listen to the enemy's threats or be distracted by enemy attack, for You are ready to deflect every arrow and turn away every foe on my behalf.

Psalms 119:41-45

May Your unfailing love come to me, Lord, Your salvation, according to Your promise; then I can answer anyone who taunts me, for I trust in Your word. Never take Your word of truth from my mouth, for I have put my hope in Your laws. I will always obey Your law, for ever and ever. I will walk about in freedom, for I have sought out Your precepts.

I cling to Your word, Lord, which alone brings me health and wholeness. I turn from the voices that try to make me doubt Your promise and question Your goodness. Remind me to declare Your truth when the enemy taunts and tempts me to doubt Your desire to heal me. I rest on Your word and Your intention to bring me through in total victory.

Psalm 57:2-3
I cry out to God Most High, to God, who vindicates me. He sends from heaven and saves me, rebuking those who hotly pursue me - God sends forth His love and His faithfulness.

Thank You, Lord, for saving me from the enemy's attempts to destroy my faith and kill my body! Even when I feel attacked, You send forth Your love and Your faithfulness. You are the one who vindicates me and champions my victory and defeat over the enemy's schemes.

Isaiah 41:10
So do not fear, for I am with you; do not be dismayed, for I am your God. I will strengthen you and help you; I will uphold you with My righteous right hand.

I will not give in to fear when new symptoms arise, or setbacks occur. I will not be surprised when the enemy turns up the heat, for it is only a reminder that Your presence and power are working! I receive Your strength and courage to stand firm in my resolve and in the promise of Your word. I rest in the palm of Your hand and trust in Your righteous decrees over my life.

Isaiah 54:17
No weapon forged against you will prevail, and you will refute every tongue that accuses you. This is the heritage of the servants of the Lord, and this is their vindication from Me, declares the Lord.

When my resolve begins to weaken, Lord, remind me of Your authority and power over every scheme of the enemy! When I have placed my confidence in You, nothing can stand in the way of Your healing and deliverance. This is Your covenant promise to me as Your child. You delight in defeating my enemies and setting me free from every trap and destroying every weapon that has been forged against me. Thank You for vindicating me and shielding me from all of the enemy's plans.

John 10:10

The thief comes only to steal and kill and destroy; I have come that they may have life, and have it to the full.

I refuse and renounce the plans of the enemy to steal my health, kill my body, and destroy my faith! I am filled with the Spirit and power of God and a vessel for His life giving waters to flow. I receive the fullness of the Spirit and speak abundant life and blessing over every joint, ligament, organ, and vein. My body is a temple of the Holy Spirit, filled to the fullest with life, blessing, and supernatural strength.

Acts 4:29-31

"Now, Lord, consider their threats and enable Your servants to speak Your word with great boldness. Stretch out Your hand to heal and perform signs and wonders through the name of Your holy servant Jesus." After they prayed, the place where they were meeting was shaken. And they were all filled with the Holy Spirit and spoke the word of God boldly.

I receive now the infilling power of the Holy Spirit with which to rebuke and displace all the threats of the enemy against my health and well-being. Grant me even greater boldness, Lord, to speak Your Word without hesitation. Even in the midst of setbacks and disappointments, I thank You for sending Your healing grace with signs and wonders that will cause others to see Your glory and the power of Your Spirit.

2 Corinthians 10:5

We demolish arguments and every pretension that sets itself up against the knowledge of God, and we take captive every thought to make it obedient to Christ.

Holy Spirit, reveal to me every lie and twisted idea that is coming from the enemy so that I can demolish it with Your truth. I call forth every thought and feeling that is opposed to the goodness of God and His healing power to come into submission now, in Jesus' name. I refuse to entertain any thought that does not reflect God's design and desire to see me healed and whole. I bring those thoughts and feelings to the cross and crucify their influence in my life. Thank You, Jesus, for revealing Your truth to displace the lies and reinforcing the power of Your love in my life.

James 4:7
Submit yourselves, then, to God. Resist the devil, and he will flee from you.

Today, Lord, I yield myself to You once again. I submit to Your protection, Your guidance, and Your direction. I refuse to entertain doubt or fear and resist the devil's attempts to rob me of my peace. I say to the workers of darkness to leave my presence now as I come under the shadow of God's wings and His providential care. I belong to You, Lord, and the devil will have no hold on me!

NOTES

He is Perfect Love

Lamentations 3:22-24

Because of the Lord's great love we are not consumed, for His compassions never fail. They are new every morning; great is Your faithfulness. I say to myself, "The Lord is my portion; therefore, I will wait for Him."

I will not be overwhelmed by my condition or symptoms, nor will I cave in to my weaknesses. They will not consume me, for Your love is greater, Lord! Every day I wake up, You are there to meet me with great compassion and a desire to heal me. You are faithful to Your Word and always keep Your promises. I will wait for the full manifestation of Your Word, knowing that Your ways are always the highest and always the best.

Psalms 91:14-16

"Because he loves me," says the Lord, "I will rescue him; I will protect him, for he acknowledges My name. He will call on Me, and I will answer him; I will be with him in trouble, I will deliver him and honor him. With long life I will satisfy him and show him My salvation."

You reward those who love You, Lord. When You hear us call Your name, You immediately respond with great care and compassion. You are with me in trouble and promise to deliver me and honor me. You have promised me long life as a result of trusting in You and consistently calling on Your name. I receive Your protection and provision and will continue to look to You first and foremost for all my needs.

Psalms 107:19-21

Then they cried to the Lord in their trouble, and He saved them from their distress. He sent out His word and healed them; He rescued them from the grave. Let them give thanks to the Lord for His unfailing love and His wonderful deeds for mankind.

Your love, O Lord, compels You to respond to those who cry out to You in trouble. You deliver me from my distress because of Your unconditional love and concern. You send out Your Word to heal and rescue me from the grave. Your love never fails to respond to my needs. When in doubt, help me to see how You have answered my prayers and come to my side without delay or hesitation.

Psalm 136:12
...with a mighty hand and outstretched arm; His love endures forever.

Your love never quits, and it never stops giving! There is no end to Your determination in demonstrating the fullness of Your love to me. Let me see Your outstretched arm that is raised on my behalf. Open my eyes and heart to see how much You are already working on my behalf, Lord!

Psalms 138:8
The Lord will vindicate me; Your love, Lord, endures forever - do not abandon the works of Your hands.

You love me so completely, Lord, that You will vindicate my cause and free me from my enemy that wants me weak and sick. Thank You for not giving me over to the pain, but remaining steadfast in securing my freedom, my wholeness, and my joy.

Psalm 144:1-3
Praise be to the Lord my Rock, who trains my hands for war, my fingers for battle. He is my loving God and my fortress, my stronghold and my deliverer, my shield, in whom I take refuge, who subdues peoples under me. Lord, what are human beings that You care for them, mere mortals that You think of them?

Father, You have given me all the tools I need to stand in this battle and fight off the enemy. You have put in my hands Your sword of truth with which to demolish the lies that are aimed at making me sick and weak. You have put within me the capacity to speak Your name with power and authority and not shrink back from the adversary's challenge. You are the One who guards me, shields me, covers me, and cheers me on in this warfare. Thank You for standing with me as we slay the enemy together!

Jeremiah 30:17

"But I will restore you to health and heal your wounds," declares the Lord, "because you are called an outcast, Zion for whom no one cares."

Thank You, Lord, for caring for me and picking me up when I fall. You promise to restore me to health and heal my wounds because of Your great love and compassion. Thank You for being such a faithful Father.

Romans 5:3-5

Not only so, but we also glory in our sufferings because we know that suffering produces perseverance; perseverance, character; and character, hope. And hope does not put us to shame, because God's love has been poured out into our hearts through the Holy Spirit, who has been given to us.

Lord, You use even my suffering for my good and for Your glory. Pour out Your love into my heart through Your Holy Spirit so I can embrace and receive Your perseverance, Your character, and Your hope. I do not have these on my own, but through the power of Your Holy Spirit, I receive the fullness of Your love. It's Your unending love that imparts to me the character and perseverance of Christ and the everlasting hope that only You can provide.

NOTES

He Has a Plan for Every Healing

Jeremiah 29:11
"For I know the plans I have for you," declares the Lord, "plans to prosper you and not to harm you, plans to give you hope and a future.

I praise You for Your perfect plans for my life and for this current season of healing. You have already prepared ahead for this journey and made provision for every challenge. You have not changed Your mind in blessing me with a bright future and in fulfilling the call on my life. You never seek to harm me, but only allow that which will strengthen me and make me even more fruitful and productive on this side of eternity. Thank You for Your perfect plans!

Psalms 107:20
He sent out His word and healed them; He rescued them from the grave.

It only takes a Word from You, Lord, to rescue me from the enemy's grip. It only takes a Word from Your mouth to utterly shatter the enemy's hold on my life and rescue me from the pit. Remind me of the words You have already spoken over my life so that I can declare them out loud as a reminder to my adversaries. Thank You for the power of Your Word that destroys sickness and disease and sets me free.

Isaiah 53:5
But He was pierced for our transgressions, He was crushed for our iniquities; the punishment that brought us peace was on Him, and by His wounds we are healed.

Your work on the cross was complete, Lord. You didn't forget anything. You took on my sins, my weaknesses, my frailties, and all my sicknesses and diseases. You abolished all their hold on me and because of Your sacrifice, You purchased my complete healing and restoration. You did this for me, Lord, and I receive this gift of love and appropriate the power of Your blood to do its finishing work.

Matthew 9:5-8

"Which is easier: to say, 'Your sins are forgiven,' or to say, 'Get up and walk'? But I want you to know that the Son of Man has authority on earth to forgive sins." So, He said to the paralyzed man, "Get up, take your mat and go home." Then the man got up and went home. When the crowd saw this, they were filled with awe; and they praised God, who had given such authority to man.

Lord, with the same power that You forgive all my sins, You also heal my body. May I remember the power You have given me over sin and its similar power over sickness and disease. What You did on the cross covered it all. Show me if I have forgotten the power of Your blood that has cleansed me from sin so that I can apply its same power over my body, mind, and soul.

Matthew 9:35

Jesus went through all the towns and villages, teaching in their synagogues, proclaiming the good news of the kingdom and healing every disease and sickness.

When You heal, You also proclaim the good news of the Kingdom and teach Your people how to live. Help me to embrace Your life-giving truths that will keep me for the long haul and empower me to walk in divine health and well-being. Thank You for covering ALL sicknesses and diseases and not leaving any out of the equation. Thank You for fresh revelation of who You are and Your purposes for my life that will increase my faith to appropriate my healing.

Luke 6:19

And the people all tried to touch Him, because power was coming from Him and healing them all.

I want to touch You, Lord, and feel the power of Your healing presence in my life. Draw me closer to You on a daily basis so I can touch the hem of Your garment and receive all that You have for me. Your power never turns off, and Your love never ends. Remind me to come close, each and every day, so that I can receive of the overflow coming out of heaven and the reality of Your presence.

Luke 8:53-55
They laughed at Him, knowing that she was dead. But He took her by the hand and said, "My child, get up!" Her spirit returned, and at once she stood up. Then Jesus told them to give her something to eat.

Lord, may I never get to the point where I don't believe that Your healing power can work. You bring the dead back to life! May my heart always be filled with faith in Your goodness and love and be set to receive the fulness of Your promise. Give me Your joy with which to laugh in the presence of my enemies and declare the goodness of the Lord.

Luke 13:12-13
When Jesus saw her, He called her forward and said to her, "Woman, you are set free from your infirmity." Then He put His hands on her, and immediately she straightened up and praised God.

Help me to listen for Your voice, Lord, so that I can immediately respond to Your invitations. Thank You for setting me free from infirmity and touching me with Your power. Thank You for seeing my need and calling me out so that I can be set free. Keep me alert at all times to the promptings of Your Spirit so that I can receive all that You have planned for me.

Luke 17:14
When He saw them, He said, "Go, show yourselves to the priests." And as they went, they were cleansed.

Open my eyes, Lord, to all the ways in which You may want to heal me. Show me if I have placed my expectations on the wrong thing instead of trusting Your plans and purposes. The healing I seek is not just about me, but about many others who are watching and needing a touch from You. May my obedience bring You pleasure and may my response to Your directives bring the healing I desire and the glory You deserve.

John 4:50-53
"Go," Jesus replied, "your son will live." The man took Jesus at his word and departed. While he was still on the way, his servants met him with the news that his boy was living. When he inquired as to the time when

his son got better, they said to him, "Yesterday, at one in the afternoon, the fever left him." Then the father realized that this was the exact time at which Jesus had said to him, "Your son will live." So, he and his whole household believed.

May I take You at Your word, Lord, and immediately trust in Your response to my plea. You know exactly what I am facing and have already determined its outcome. Help me to respond quickly to Your instructions, knowing that Your love is leading the way. You have determined to not only bless me and my household, but others who are watching our journey. Thank You for Your perfect ways of healing!

Acts 5:16
Crowds gathered also from the towns around Jerusalem, bringing their sick and those tormented by impure spirits, and all of them were healed.

Lord, sometimes You heal in crowds because of the collective hunger and faith. Direct me to those places where I can gather with the saints and be encouraged and empowered by the corporate faith of fellow believers. Thank You for not only healing the sickness in my body but delivering me from any evil spirits or enemy influence. Make me more alert to the kind of healing I truly need and direct my steps so that I will recognize where You are working.

Romans 8:2
Because through Christ Jesus the law of the Spirit who gives life has set you free from the law of sin and death.

I have been set free from the law of sin and death. I do not have to submit to sickness, disease, and the work of the enemy! I am a recipient of the Spirit of life who has released me from the entrapments of my spiritual adversary. I live under a new covenant which promises me life, health, and well-being as I now follow the law of the Spirit.

Romans 10:17
Consequently, faith comes from hearing the message, and the message is heard through the Word about Christ.

I want to increase my faith in You, Lord. I know that can only happen when I feed my soul and spirit with good things. Direct my attention to messages, both written and verbal, that will build my confidence in Your Word and in Your character. Show me how to properly feed myself on truth and nourish my faith so it can fully reflect Your heart, Your character, and Your ultimate purpose for my life.

2 Corinthians 9:8
And God is able to bless you abundantly, so that in all things, at all times, having all that you need, you will abound in every good work.

You've planned ahead for me, God. There is never a time when You don't provide a solution or give me a step to follow that will bring me closer to the answers I seek. You delight in my success and are always there to give me whatever I need for the day's tasks. I declare that I will abound in every good work that You have purposed for me and that I will succeed in this journey of faith.

2 Corinthians 12:9
But He said to me, "My grace is sufficient for you, for My power is made perfect in weakness." Therefore, I will boast all the more gladly about my weaknesses so that Christ's power may rest on me.

Even when I feel weak, it's only an opportunity for Your presence and power to take over. You know my limits, Father. You know what I can and can't do. But Your perfect love rushes in to pick me up and carry me through those times when I can't walk on my own. It is Your power and Your love that will become even more evident to me and those around me as I daily surrender to You.

Philippians 4:19
And my God will meet all your needs according to the riches of His glory in Christ Jesus.

Lord, You meet ALL of my needs. Not just some of them. Help me to rightly distinguish between my wants and my needs. Forgive me for not recognizing Your provision and only focusing on what I want. I trust You to know exactly what I need and how I need it. You don't miss a thing. May I have Your eyes and Your ears to perceive Your provision in all things and give You the glory for answering my plea.

1 Thessalonians 5:23-24

May God Himself, the God of peace, sanctify you through and through. May your whole spirit, soul and body be kept blameless at the coming of our Lord Jesus Christ. The one who calls you is faithful, and He will do it.

I know it is Your desire to heal my mind, soul, and spirit, even more than my body. This is Your goal, and I yield to Your process of sanctifying me through and through. May my faith hold fast in Your faithfulness to complete my journey so that I will be whole.

James 5:13-16

Is anyone among you in trouble? Let them pray. Is anyone happy? Let them sing songs of praise. Is anyone among you sick? Let them call the elders of the church to pray over them and anoint them with oil in the name of the Lord. And the prayer offered in faith will make the sick person well; the Lord will raise them up. If they have sinned, they will be forgiven. Therefore, confess your sins to each other and pray for each other so that you may be healed. The prayer of a righteous person is powerful and effective.

Lord, You have taught us how to ask for healing and how to rightly prepare our hearts. Show me any way in which I am harboring unforgiveness towards someone. Reveal any way in which bitterness of soul or disappointment is hindering healing in my life. I am willing to confess these faults before my brothers and sisters and ask forgiveness to clear my conscience and prepare the way for Your healing grace to flow. Increase my desire to pray with others concerning the issues of my heart and humble myself in a way that makes room for You to move on my behalf.

1 Peter 2:24

He Himself bore our sins in His body on the cross, so that we might die to sin and live for righteousness; by His wounds you have been healed.

You desire complete healing of the soul, mind, and body. This is in order for us to be fully like You and walk in holiness and righteousness. Sickness and disease do not represent who You are, Lord. You desire for us to be a walking demonstration of the life of Christ which is free from sin, sickness, and every curse of the enemy. Thank You for going to the cross and making a way for us to be just like You.

NOTES

He is Always Good

1 Chronicles 16:34
Give thanks to the Lord, for He is good; His love endures forever.

Because of Your unending goodness, Lord, I will give You thanks. Because of Your unfailing love, I will thank you every day for how You are at work in my life. Even on the days when I don't feel well or am discouraged and weak, You are still good and Your love has not changed. Thank You for being so constant – and so good!

Psalms 16:2
I say to the Lord, "You are my Lord; apart from You I have no good thing."

Even as I thank You for sending me help through practical means and support, my healing ultimately rests in You, Lord. Nothing is as good as Your supernatural healing touch and Your power at work in my life. I desire to see even more of Your goodness revealed in my mortal body so that others can see the amazing God You truly are.

Psalms 23:6
Surely Your goodness and love will follow me all the days of my life, and I will dwell in the house of the Lord forever.

Even when sickness or discomfort seem to be my daily companions, Your goodness and love are greater. Every day Your goodness follows me and watches over me. Open my eyes to see how Your goodness is at work in this process and to recognize how much You care about my condition and will never leave me or forsake me.

Psalm 30:2
Lord my God, I called to You for help, and You healed me.

Just like a great Father, You are right there to answer me whenever I call upon Your name. Even if I can't feel You or detect Your presence, it is Your goodness that guarantees Your help to come. You are the first one to respond to my need, and I thank You for being so good to me!

Psalms 31:19

How abundant are the good things that You have stored up for those who fear You, that You bestow in the sight of all, on those who take refuge in You.

Everything You do, Lord, is over the top! Your goodness is so great and so abundant, it releases all the healing grace that is needed to be whole and well. As I look to You as my Healer, I receive all of Your goodness and all of Your provision to be totally healed and set free. I believe there are even better things that You have stored up for me and I look forward to the days ahead!

Psalms 34:8

Taste and see that the Lord is good; blessed is the one who takes refuge in Him.

Lord, forgive me when I start complaining and miss Your working in my life. Help me to see Your activity in this process and Your goodness in every step. As I take refuge in You, I want to taste even more of Your goodness and feast on Your never-ending supply of love and care.

Psalms 119:68

You are good, and what You do is good; teach me Your decrees.

Lord, You can do nothing wrong, nor can You do anything that is not good for me. All of your plans for my life are good and Your goodness is at work, even now, in the midst of pain and discomfort. Teach me more of Your Word and reveal even more of who You really are so that I can know Your goodness more fully.

Psalms 142:5-7

I cry to You, Lord; I say, "You are my refuge, my portion in the land of the living." Listen to my cry, for I am in desperate need; rescue me from those who pursue me, for they are too strong for me. Set me free from my prison, that I may praise Your name. Then the righteous will gather about me because of Your goodness to me.

Thank You for listening to my cries for help, Lord. You never fail to rescue those who call upon Your name. You set me free from a prison of doubt and fear and set me high above my enemies. It is because You are a good, good Father that You do this for me. Thank You for loving me unconditionally and always intervening on my behalf. Thank You for my testimony to come that will demonstrate Your goodness to all.

Psalms 143:10
Teach me to do Your will, for You are my God; may Your good Spirit lead me on level ground.

Teach me what Your will is for my life and for this journey, Lord. Holy Spirit, lead me to healing. Lead me every step of the way and show me what to do. Help me not wander from Your path and keep me alert to all of Your instructions so that I can see the full manifestation of healing in my body, soul, mind, and spirit. In Jesus' name!

Lamentations 3:25-26
The Lord is good to those whose hope is in Him, to the one who seeks Him; it is good to wait quietly for the salvation of the Lord.

Lord, forgive me for my impatience. Help me to stay in a place of hope and to always trust in Your desire to heal me. I will wait for how and when this happens and will quiet my anxious thoughts and needless concerns. I will continue to seek You in this process and take Your lead in this journey, knowing that I will eventually see the salvation and healing of the Lord!

Nahum 1:7
The Lord is good, a refuge in times of trouble. He cares for those who trust in Him.

As I trust in You, Lord, You care for my every need. When I'm in trouble and am unsure of my future, You are my stronghold and security. Your goodness overshadows my life, and I receive Your presence and peace that will bring me into complete healing and wholeness. Your goodness is greater than any sickness or disease, and I praise You as my gracious Heavenly Father.

Matthew 7:11
If you, then, though you are evil, know how to give good gifts to your children, how much more will your Father in heaven give good gifts to those who ask Him!

Because You are a good Father, You do not give bad things to Your children. You want us to ask You for things, because You delight in giving good gifts to Your sons and daughters. I desire healing in my body, Lord, and I believe You are working on my behalf so that I can receive this amazing gift.

John 14:27
Peace, I leave with you; My peace I give you. I do not give to you as the world gives. Do not let your hearts be troubled and do not be afraid.

I receive Your peace, Lord. Not the peace in knowing all the details of this journey, but simply the peace of Your presence. When You are with me, I know I can face anything, for Your presence overshadows me with an absolute confidence in Your goodness. I do not falter when Your peace engulfs me and surrounds me. May Your peace blanket my heart so that it will rest secure in Your love and goodness.

John 15:7-8
If you remain in Me and My words remain in you, ask whatever you wish, and it will be done for you. This is to My Father's glory, that you bear much fruit, showing yourselves to be My disciples.

Wow, Lord! What a promise! You say that if I remain in You and follow Your directives, I can ask anything from You as my Father, and You will grant it to me. You want me to succeed, and You want me to bear good fruit in my life. Show me how to be more consistent and faithful in spending time with You and becoming one with You. Purify my heart so that my greatest desire will not be focused on my healing but knowing YOU as my Healer.

Acts 10:38
How God anointed Jesus of Nazareth with the Holy Spirit and power, and how He went around doing good and healing all who were under the power of the devil, because God was with Him.

Jesus, You can only do good. You cannot do anything BUT good. Thank You for setting the standard when You walked the earth by healing all who were under the power of the devil. Thank You for setting me free from demonic oppression and every tormenting spirit that seeks to take me out. Your goodness and compassion are without end. I declare that no work of the devil is allowed to work in my body, soul, or mind. I say to the devil to "GET OUT in Jesus' name! I am a vessel of righteousness and declare my body off limits to any work of darkness!"

Romans 8:28

And we know that in all things God works for the good of those who love Him, who have been called according to His purpose.

Everything You do, God, is good! As I look to You for every step I take in my healing, You will make it work out for my good and for Your glory. Thank You for using everything I'm walking through to benefit me and encourage others in the future. Keep me on track so that I can fulfill all that You have planned for me. I look forward to the day when I share my testimony of healing that will open doors of healing for others!

NOTES

He's Given Us Authority

Matthew 10:1

Jesus called His twelve disciples to Him and gave them authority to drive out impure spirits and to heal every disease and sickness.

You have given all of Your followers the authority to heal every sickness and disease. You did not categorize them or qualify them, but simply said we had authority over them. This was always the standard and You've never changed it. You already paid the debt and purchased our healing on the cross. I stand in that authority now, knowing it is true and is Your perfect will.

Matthew 18:19-20

Again, truly I tell you that if two of you on earth agree about anything they ask for, it will be done for them by My Father in heaven. For where two or three gather in My name, there am I with them."

Show me who I can pray with in agreement so that Your will can be accomplished in my life. Show me who walks in Your faith and confidence for healing and can stand with me in contending for my breakthrough. Thank You for responding to those who agree with You and stand fast together for what You have already promised!

Luke 4:18-19

The Spirit of the Lord is on Me because He has anointed Me to proclaim good news to the poor. He has sent Me to proclaim freedom for the prisoners and recovery of sight for the blind, to set the oppressed free, to proclaim the year of the Lord's favor.

I have the same Spirit within me that Jesus had. I, too, have been anointed to proclaim good news over my life and proclaim freedom from the sickness and disease that has held me captive. Through the power of the Spirit, I declare blind eyes open and the lame to walk. Through the power of the Spirit within me, I rebuke oppression off of my life and declare freedom from any sickness of soul and mind. I declare that this is the year of the Lord's favor on my life, and I will see His healing presence and power like never before.

Luke 10:17-19
The seventy-two returned with joy and said, "Lord, even the demons submit to us in Your name." He replied, "I saw Satan fall like lightning from heaven. I have given you authority to trample on snakes and scorpions and to overcome all the power of the enemy; nothing will harm you."

Hallelujah! Satan has already fallen and lost the war that is being waged against me. I know that nothing can harm me because of the power and authority of Your name, Jesus. You defeated Satan at the cross and gave me the same authority to overcome every scheme and plan to destroy my life and my faith. Thank You for making me an overcomer!

Romans 8:11 (NLT)
The Spirit of God, who raised Jesus from the dead, lives in you. And just as God raised Christ Jesus from the dead, He will give life to your mortal bodies by this same Spirit living within you.

Thank you, Jesus, for sharing with me the same resurrection power that brought You out of the grave! You have given me the same authority over sickness and disease and granted me victory over death. That same wonder-working power is inside of me right now and I receive Your resurrection life into this mortal body. Raise me from this grave of sickness and show forth the power of Your love!

Romans 16:20
The God of peace will soon crush Satan under your feet. The grace of our Lord Jesus be with you.

I am walking and living by the grace of God, accessing the same power and authority of Christ Jesus, my Lord. The Prince of Peace has already gone before me and crushed Satan underneath my feet. Every attack aimed against me is subject to the weight of His judgment and the strength of His mighty foot upon the serpent's head. I have no fear of the threats, for the God of Peace is my shield and my victory.

1 John 4:4
You, dear children, are from God and have overcome them because the one who is in you is greater than the one who is in the world.

I belong to the Most High God who has all power and authority over sickness, disease, and death! You have called me an overcomer, Father, and I joyfully yield to Your Lordship with full assurance of Your ultimate authority over the enemy. I call out the enemy's lies and declare that my God is so much greater than these futile attempts to make me doubt the absolute goodness of my Lord.

NOTES

His Timing is Perfect

Ecclesiastes 3:1
There is a time for everything, and a season for every activity under the heavens.

All times are in Your hands, Lord. That means the good times as well as the challenging times. You are Lord of each time and season and Your plans are perfect throughout. You order every day and every circumstance so that my life can experience the fullness of who You are and all that You have provided for me. When I am under the shadow of Your wings, regardless of how things feel, it's always the perfect time to get to know You more fully.

Ecclesiastes 3:11
He has made everything beautiful in its time. He has also set eternity in the human heart; yet no one can fathom what God has done from beginning to end.

Even though I have experienced pain, suffering, and setback, You intend to make it all beautiful! Lord, give me an eternal perspective on my life that I can see just how much You will use all of this for my good and for Your glory. Show me how this journey will reveal things about You I never dreamed of. Give me Your eyes with which to understand how truly good and beautiful this season is and the eternal rewards that will come as a result.

Psalms 31:15
My times are in Your hands; deliver me from the hands of my enemies, from those who pursue me.

I release the timing of this healing journey to You, God. I am in the palm of Your hand and I give You permission to order every day, every experience, and every conversation. I am not my own. You are the Lord of my life and the Lord of my healing. You are the only one who can rightly determine my path and the direction I should take. Thank You for planning ahead so completely for me!

Psalms 90:12

Teach us to number our days, that we may gain a heart of wisdom.

You have allotted this time and season specifically for me, Lord. You knew ahead of time what I would face and have determined to use it all for my good. Teach me the lessons I need in this journey, not only to find greater healing, but to grow in wisdom and understanding in defeating every scheme of the devil.

Proverbs 16:9

In their hearts humans plan their course, but the Lord establishes their steps.

You know I have my own ideas about my healing, Lord! But even though I have expectations and hopes I only want what You want – and when You want it. Establish every one of my steps so that I can have a clear conscience and free heart with which to perceive Your presence. Stop me when I start to steer my own course. I relinquish any control and invite You to determine the exact timing of the complete healing I need.

Proverbs 21:5

The plans of the diligent lead to profit as surely as haste leads to poverty.

Lord, forgive me for trying to speed up this process when You may have something else to show me. May I stay faithful to Your directions and be diligent in all that You have already said. I will not be hasty or quick to judge but wait on You to fulfill all Your purposes for me in this time.

Luke 1:37

For no word from God will ever fail.

Regardless of the time or the season, Your words never fail, and You always fulfill Your promise! Forgive me for limiting Your work in assuming how and when You will heal me. Only You know what is needed to complete this journey in complete victory. Only You know how others will be impacted by my coming testimony. I trust You completely and will not doubt Your Word.

Romans 5:6
You see, at just the right time, when we were still powerless, Christ died for the ungodly.

Father, You knew the exact and perfect time when to send Your Son to the earth. Even with all that had gone before, You knew everything that had to take place in order for the biggest blessing to come in His sacrifice. In like manner, You know the exact and perfect time to reveal the fullness of Your plans for my life. You have already purposed since the foundation of the world to heal me and set me free. Thank You for the victory that is sure to come – at just the right time.

Ephesians 5:15-17
Be very careful, then, how you live - not as unwise but as wise, making the most of every opportunity because the days are evil. Therefore, do not be foolish, but understand what the Lord's will is.

Father, I pray that I will receive the most benefit possible from this time of healing. Even as my spiritual adversary seeks to discourage me in this time, help me to be wise and glean every revelation, every truth, and every insight You have in mind. May I not give in to desperation and try to abort this season of instruction and growth. May I come out with increased strength, stamina, authority, and absolute confidence in the goodness of God!

1 Peter 5:6-7
Humble yourselves, therefore, under God's mighty hand, that He may lift you up in due time. Cast all your anxiety on Him because He cares for you.

Only You know the perfect time for my breakthrough to come. Only You know all the factors that go into this process and how to sanctify and refine my heart, Lord. I yield to Your methods and means of healing in my life, knowing that You hear my cries for help and have determined to answer me fully, completely, and exactly on time.

2 Peter 3:8-9
But do not forget this one thing, dear friends: With the Lord a day is like a thousand years, and a thousand years are like a day. The Lord is not

slow in keeping His promise, as some understand slowness. Instead, He is patient with you, not wanting anyone to perish, but everyone to come to repentance.

Forgive me, Lord, for being impatient. What seems like a never-ending battle is but a blink in time from eternity's perspective. You are never slow or out of pace. You have a distinct purpose for every path I take. Help me to see Your purposes and Your plans so that this season of time will be rich in fruit and a treasure to cherish.

James 4:13-14

Now listen, you who say, "Today or tomorrow we will go to this or that city, spend a year there, carry on business and make money." Why, you do not even know what will happen tomorrow. What is your life? You are a mist that appears for a little while and then vanishes.

Forgive me, Lord, for trying to make my own plans without first consulting You. I release my own plans and ask that You give me Your blueprint for my life. Help me adjust my expectations and come into better alignment with Your ultimate purposes in this season of time.

NOTES

NOTES

He Provides All We Need

Genesis 9:3

Everything that lives and moves about will be food for you. Just as I gave you the green plants, I now give you everything.

Teach me, Lord, about all the natural remedies and medicines You have already placed within creation. Renew my mind concerning my health and how You have provided herbs and plants to benefit us and our well being. Help me to understand and utilize these tools in my healing journey.

Psalms 23:1

The Lord is my shepherd, I lack nothing.

I turn my eyes away from any seeming lack, for when You are in the picture, I lack nothing! I want to draw so close to Your heart during this time that nothing else truly matters. May my flesh not rule me, and may my human desires not overshadow the reality of Your constant presence and desire to do me good. You are my Good Shepherd and will always take care of me!

Psalms 34:10

The lions may grow weak and hungry, but those who seek the Lord lack no good thing.

I will look to You, first and foremost, for everything I need, God. Even when I look to practical solutions, I know that You are the source of everything that is good for me. You delight in giving me good things and will never let me down. You want me to seek You first. Help me to do that, knowing that Your provision will always follow.

Matthew 6:31-33

So do not worry, saying, 'What shall we eat?' or 'What shall we drink?' or 'What shall we wear?' For the pagans run after all these things, and your heavenly Father knows that you need them. But seek first His kingdom and His righteousness, and all these things will be given to you as well.

Forgive me, Lord, for worrying about the details. Forgive me for my anxious thoughts that are preoccupied with what I need and what I don't have. You have promised to provide everything I need in order to succeed and be victorious. I declare my trust in You to bring to me what I need, and when I need it. You know my concerns before I even ask! Open my eyes so that I can see Your provision and give You thanks.

Matthew 7:11
If you, then, though you are evil, know how to give good gifts to your children, how much more will your Father in heaven give good gifts to those who ask Him!

You are a good Father! You are not capable of giving Your children anything that is bad or not good for them. You delight in me asking You for help and looking to You for direction. Remind me when I forget to ask and start to complain. Remind me that we are on this journey together and You want to be a part of every step. You love to listen to my heart and are glad when I trust You as my Heavenly Father.

Romans 8:26-27
In the same way, the Spirit helps us in our weakness. We do not know what we ought to pray for, but the Spirit Himself intercedes for us through wordless groans. And He who searches our hearts knows the mind of the Spirit because the Spirit intercedes for God's people in accordance with the will of God.

Thank You, Holy Spirit, for helping me to pray. Thank You for interceding on my behalf and giving me a spiritual language with which to pour out my heart. I confess I do not always know what to pray, but because of the gift of Your Spirit, you give me the ability to communicate God's perfect will for my life when I pray by the Spirit. Increase my capacity to use this gift as a viable means towards my healing.

2 Corinthians 9:8
And God is able to bless you abundantly, so that in all things, at all times, having all that you need, you will abound in every good work.

I receive the abundance of Your House, Lord. I know You will lead me to all the help I need, whether it's information, connections, revelations, or practical assistance. You will not leave anything out! For You not only provide for me but want to shower me with blessing so that I can reveal Your goodness to those around me.

Philippians 4:11-13

I am not saying this because I am in need, for I have learned to be content whatever the circumstances. I know what it is to be in need, and I know what it is to have plenty. I have learned the secret of being content in any and every situation, whether well fed or hungry, whether living in plenty or in want. I can do all this through Him who gives me strength.

May I have the same testimony as Paul, to be content in any and every situation. May I share his secret in being satisfied with Your goodness and presence, even when things may appear dark. For You not only provide me with practical help and spiritual aid but provide me supernatural grace to persevere and not quit. You are my strength and the source of my faith. Thank You for Your provision of amazing grace!

Philippians 4:19

And my God will meet all your needs according to the riches of His glory in Christ Jesus.

Lord, help me to see every provision You are making for me to secure my healing. Show me every spiritual truth I need to know and lead me to the right information that is practical and useful to live in health and well being for the long term. Bring to me every resource that will be helpful, as well as every divine connection and appointment that will further Your purposes and encourage my own faith.

Colossians 1:11-14

Being strengthened with all power according to His glorious might so that you may have great endurance and patience, and giving joyful thanks to the Father, who has qualified you to share in the inheritance of His holy people in the kingdom of light. For He has rescued us from the dominion of darkness and brought us into the kingdom of the Son He loves, in whom we have redemption, the forgiveness of sins.

Thank You for giving me all power and strength to overcome the works of darkness. I receive Your grace to endure and be patient, and to be thankful in this healing journey because of the inheritance that You have secured for me. You have brought me out of darkness and into the light because I am Yours and part of Your everlasting Kingdom of joy and peace. Because I am Yours, You have given me everything I need to secure my blessing.

2 Thessalonians 3:3
But the Lord is faithful, and He will strengthen you and protect you from the evil one.

Your faithfulness always gives me strength, Lord. By trusting in You, I can receive a daily dose of supernatural strength to continue this healing journey and know that I am protected from the evil one. Help me to stay so connected to You that there is no room for the arrows of the enemy to penetrate the wall of protection You provide. Thank You for Your provision!

2 Peter 1:3
His divine power has given us everything we need for a godly life through our knowledge of Him who called us by His own glory and goodness.

You not only paid for my sins and my sickness, You have also provided everything I need in this life. You have given me a Kingdom account from which I can withdraw! Open my eyes to see Your provision, not only in Your Word, but through interactions with others. Teach me about all You have given me so that I can appropriate them in my life, starting today.

Jude 1:20
But you, dear friends, by building yourselves up in your most holy faith and praying in the Holy Spirit.

Thank You, Lord, for giving us Your Holy Spirit with which to communicate and intercede. I receive the language of the Spirit so I can adequately convey all that is required for this healing process. Fill me afresh with Holy Spirit, along with His language and tongue. Remind me to use this spiritual language as a means of building myself up in faith and hope.

NOTES

NOTES

He Rewards Our Obedience

Exodus 15:26
He said, "If you listen carefully to the Lord your God and do what is right in His eyes, if you pay attention to His commands and keep all His decrees, I will not bring on you any of the diseases I brought on the Egyptians, for I am the Lord, who heals you."

You are the God who heals me! When I obey Your Word and follow Your directives, You provide protection and safety against the attacks of the enemy over my life. Show me any way in which I've overlooked a directive or failed to obey Your Word so that I can be assured of this providential protection over my life.

Deuteronomy 5:33
Walk in obedience to all that the Lord your God has commanded you, so that you may live and prosper and prolong your days in the land that you will possess.

Your Word consistently says that You will bless all who walk in obedience to Your commands. You want us to live long lives and be healthy. Lead my heart so that I will always desire to do Your will and not my own. May I be faithful to Your words and willingly follow where You lead me.

1 Samuel 15:22
But Samuel replied: "Does the Lord delight in burnt offerings and sacrifices as much as in obeying the Lord? To obey is better than sacrifice, and to heed is better than the fat of rams.

Show me, Lord, if I have tried to earn Your blessing or my healing because of good works. I know that You value my obedience much more than any seeming sacrifice I make. Help me to be faithful to what You say and not let my flesh try to rule. I trust Your plans for my healing more than I trust in my ability to work for it.

Proverbs 4:20-22
My son, pay attention to what I say; turn your ear to My words. Do not let them out of your sight, keep them within your heart; for they are life to those who find them and health to one's whole body.

There is blessing in obedience and healing in Your Word! You say that when I turn my ear towards You and stay attentive to Your directions, Your words will positively affect my physical body, mind, and soul. Like medicine, Your Word brings life and health. Everything You say brings life and life abundant! Teach me to pursue Your words even more so that I might speak them out and bring even greater healing to my life.

Isaiah 1:19
If you are willing and obedient, you will eat the good things of the land.

You promise me good things when I follow You and obey. You don't just want my obedience, though. You want my heart! I give You my heart and ask You to continue to direct it so that I desire what You desire and want what You want. I am willing to do things Your way and believe that You will let me see and taste that You are good!

Jeremiah 7:23
But I gave them this command: Obey Me, and I will be your God and you will be My people. Walk in obedience to all I command you, that it may go well with you.

I want to be well – spirit, soul, and body! Keep me sensitive to Your voice and Your Word so that I can follow without delay. Thank You, Lord, for blessing my life with Your goodness as I follow Your commands. Your Word brings life and health and is good for me! All of Your commands bring blessing, and I choose to walk in Your ways.

Luke 11:28
He replied, "Blessed rather are those who hear the word of God and obey it."

You call me blessed when I not only hear Your Word but obey it. I believe that means physical blessing as well as spiritual. You want me blessed! Help me to be a doer of Your Word and not just a hearer. May I follow Your words so that I can see the fruit of obedience in my life.

John 14:23

Jesus replied, "Anyone who loves Me will obey My teaching. My Father will love them, and We will come to them and make Our home with them.

Lord, I long for a greater measure of Your presence on this journey. May I embrace Your teachings and Your Word and walk them out on a daily basis. I know Your delight is in us walking together and building a stronger relationship. I want You to be at home with me and overshadow me with Your presence. For where Your presence is, there is peace, and there is power to heal.

1 John 5:3-4

In fact, this is love for God: to keep His commands. And His commands are not burdensome, for everyone born of God overcomes the world. This is the victory that has overcome the world, even our faith.

Your commands and directions are not only for my good, Lord – they are easy when I obey out of love. You will not place a burden on me, You simply ask me to trust You. Because You have assured me of victory over sickness and disease, I delight to do exactly what You tell me to do. I follow Your lead, not because I have to, but because I want to. I trust Your care and concern for my health and well being.

NOTES

He Blesses the Fear of the Lord

Psalm 3:7-8
Do not be wise in your own eyes; fear the Lord and shun evil. This will bring health to your body and nourishment to your bones.

Forgive me, Lord, when I have looked to my own wisdom and understanding to bring healing in my life. Forgive me for when I have taken Your presence and Word for granted and not walked in a godly fear of the Lord. Show me any way in which I have looked to the flesh or allowed the enemy entrance into my thoughts and imagination. I choose Your ways over my own and refuse to give the enemy a foothold. Thank You for nourishing my bones and body when I walk in the fear of the Lord.

Psalms 31:19
How abundant are the good things that You have stored up for those who fear You, that You bestow in the sight of all, on those who take refuge in You.

As I remember Your rule and reign in my life, I also remember Your goodness and abundance. You store up good things for those who humble themselves before You and worship You alone. Thank You for being so good to me. Thank You for Your gift of healing in my life and being so generous in love. This is Who You are!

Proverbs 10:27
The fear of the Lord adds length to life, but the years of the wicked are cut short.

You say that the fear of the Lord will add more years to my life! Thank You for extending our lives when we choose to honor Your Name and obey Your Word. Help me to be faithful in this and to be a good steward of all You have given me. Thank You for Your promise of a long and healthy life!

Proverbs 14:27
The fear of the Lord is a fountain of life, turning a person from the snares of death.

I want the rivers of Your Spirit to flow through me and give me life! I welcome the fear of the Lord to open that fountain and pour over my being, both spiritually and physically. In honoring You and revering You as Lord and King, You promise to release those life-giving waters that have the power to heal and restore everything in my life. Thank You for Your fountain of life!

Proverbs 19:23
The fear of the Lord leads to life; then one rests content, untouched by trouble.

You are the Giver of life as we acknowledge Your rule and sovereignty. I can rest content when I walk in the fear of the Lord because of Your divine protection surrounding me. Thank You that no harm can get to me when I fear no other gods but You.

Proverbs 22:4
Humility is the fear of the Lord; its wages are riches and honor and life.

Expose any pride in my life, Lord, so that I can lay it down and reset my heart towards You. Forgive me for any way in which I have not honored You or given You first place. Your promises are incredible for those who humble themselves before You. Thank You for giving me riches, honor, and life according to Your Word. You are not only Savior, but Lord of my life!

Malachi 4:2
But for you who revere My name, the sun of righteousness will rise with healing in its rays. And you will go out and frolic like well-fed calves.

Lord, I honor You and believe in the power of Your name to defeat sickness and death. As I declare the righteousness of Jesus in my life, I receive the life-giving flow of Your blood that carries healing and blessing. I speak to my body to receive the fullness of healing and to be filled with life, blessing, and a fullness of joy that refreshes and restores my life and being.

Luke 12:4-5
I tell you, My friends, do not be afraid of those who kill the body and after that can do no more. But I will show you whom you should fear: Fear Him who, after your body has been killed, has authority to throw you into hell. Yes, I tell you, fear Him.

Lord, this is a stern reminder that these bodies are only temporary. Even as I contend for my physical healing, it is Your priority that my soul is healed and my spirit pure. May I rejoice in the state of my heart more than in the state of my body! Forgive me for placing too much emphasis on physical things and not remembering the eternal significance of my walk and choosing You as Lord.

NOTES

Additional Ammunition for Healing

Prayer of Deliverance from Covid

No weapon that is fashioned against you shall succeed, and you shall refute every tongue that rises against you in judgment. This is the heritage of the servants of the Lord and their vindication from me, declares the Lord. (Isaiah 54:17 ESV)

COVID19 changed the world. What started as a dangerous virus quickly grew into a global pandemic killing untold numbers. As time has gone on and more data and research has come out, the uncomfortable reality has been found that this was no ordinary virus. Not only was it manufactured – it was engineered – by very wicked people. Specifically designed to inflict millions of innocent people with death and destruction, this "plandemic" is now being called a bioweapon by many who have followed its path. Whistleblowers and truth tellers have been working ceaselessly to expose the dark side of this global attack and bring the perpetrators to justice.

Many believers have already been standing in faith for the Lord to protect and shield us from this plague from hell. We have learned to guard our hearts and minds and put on the full armor of God to combat this unseen enemy. Yet, on my own journey of healing the Lord revealed that there was not only a need for spiritual protection from this plague – but deliverance. He said this was "demonically engineered" with the sole intent of placing curses and death upon all who were infected. So, whether it is Covid, the vaccines, or even possible shedding that new evidence is now showing, the root source is the same. This scourge has been a tool of the enemy to steal, kill, and destroy.

This was a shocking revelation, and though my husband and I had already prayed "against" Covid and any negative results on our bodies, we had never treated it as demonic. And though neither of us took the vaccine, we have been around many other innocent victims who did. I had already wondered if some of my own unusual physical symptoms might be related. As soon as I began to pray a prayer of deliverance and rebuke the evil spirits attached to Covid, I immediately began to feel the positive effects. I was stunned. And yet, it confirmed the devices of the enemy and the power of our authority in Christ to override them.

Below is a prayer for any who have had Covid, taken the vaccine, or felt the negative effects of possible shedding from others. Though I don't believe everyone will have the same experience in praying this prayer, nor has everyone been affected the same way, I encourage you to use this prayer as another powerful tool against the enemy's schemes.

Prayer for Deliverance from COVID

Father, in the name of Jesus, I come to appropriate the blood of Christ over my life, my body, my soul, and my mind due to coming in contact with COVID19. I come to break any and all curses associated with this demonic plague and break free of any claim the enemy has on me as a result. I renounce COVID19 and its negative effects on my body, my soul, and my mind. I declare that the curses attached to the COVID virus are null and void of any power to do me harm. I cancel the assignment of COVID against my life and renounce its hold. Forgive me, Lord, for any agreement I may have initially had in believing this disease was "normal" and that any associated vaccine was "safe." I cut ties with those agreements and sever any legal claim the enemy has due to me being infected and impacted by this deadly virus.

I renounce any demons that came attached to COVID and command them to leave my body, now, in the name of Jesus. I ask you, Lord, to remove all spike proteins, nanoparticles, graphene oxide, PEG, and aluminum oxide and every other destructive chemical and element from my body from COVID19, either in the virus, through the vaccine, or coming into contact with someone else who was vaccinated. I speak to my blood that it be completely cleansed by the blood of Jesus and for all blockages and clots to be removed now. I declare that my blood is clear of any toxins or poisons and that it flows without hindrance throughout my entire being.

I cancel any negative side effects of COVID19 and command all demons associated with these symptoms to leave in Jesus' name. I declare my body is the temple of the Holy Spirit and declare every organ, muscle, and tissue to be fully restored according to God's intended design. Angels, come and clear my body of any unclean spirit or demonic attachment that is hiding or seeking to stay. Come and breathe a fresh wind of the Spirit of God to clear me of all fog and chaos and clear my head. I declare that I have the mind of Christ and have clarity, alertness, and full energy and capacity to think, discern, and perceive by the Spirit of God.

I speak to my body to be fully healed and whole, free of any and all associations, contracts, or agreements with COVID along with its variants and vaccines. I claim the promises of Psalm 91 to be a habitation of the Lord's presence and protected from any evil that seeks entrance. Thank you, Lord, for freedom and deliverance from the enemy's plans. Guide me to health and right choices in the days ahead that I might walk in fullness of strength and soundness of mind.

I also pray for others who have been impacted by these demonic devices and extend Your grace and mercy so that each might find healing and restoration in Jesus' name. Grant us the wisdom to recognize future threats and stand in the authority You have given us. May we as believers testify to Your healing power and may we be agents of deliverance and salvation to the lost and hurting. To God be all the glory, both now and forevermore! AMEN.

NOTES

The Power of Forgiveness to Release Healing

This testimony is from Gail Fleming, Care Pastor at Eden Movement in Newcastle, Washington, and prayer leader for their Healing and Deliverance Team. She shares how they are seeing forgiveness as a major factor in releasing healing and deliverance:

> We have people come from all over our area looking for deliverance. Through the course of learning about deliverance we have found about 75% of the people who come are needing release from unforgiveness towards someone. Now we ask everyone who comes before we pray "Is there anyone you need to forgive?" Most of the time the answer is yes!
>
> When we neglect to forgive, it can become an open door for the enemy to come and go as he pleases. The spirit of unforgiveness never travels alone. It brings along resentment, bitterness, anger, and judgement. We take people through a simple prayer of forgiving and releasing those who may have hurt them. Then we have them repent for holding unforgiveness in their hearts, and all sins associated with it. Once they have closed the door we have them renounce this very sin. After that, we simply agree with Holy Spirit for spiritual cleansing. Most of the time, not always, the person receiving prayer says they feel a lot lighter and the atmosphere feels clean.
>
> Sometimes, their healing follows immediately after the prayer. One lady whose left side of her face was frozen, immediately smiled and was released from a demon of torment. Another lady said she knew she was delivered because the horrible thoughts she was having disappeared. Often times it's a betrayal, and for me personally, once forgiveness was given the torment ended. One lady had cancer and walked away completely healed. Another lady did not get her healing, but walked away that night free from unforgiveness, ready to meet Jesus. There are not

just a few miracles like this, but many miracles almost every Tuesday night as we see God's delivering hand at work.

In Matthew 18:35, Jesus said "My heavenly Father will also do the same to every one of you if each of you does not forgive his brother from your heart." The king had forgiven a slave a large debt, and the slave despised the forgiveness he received by not forgiving a fellow slave who owed him a small amount of debt. So, the King put him in prison and loosed the tormentors. Unforgiveness is serious. Some people have a hard time forgiving those who have hurt them. But if they had an inkling of what God has forgiven them, they would quickly forgive and repent of holding any hard feelings towards a brother or sister in the Lord - including family members who might not be saved, or anyone who has ever hurt them. The devil wants us to play with unforgiveness by analyzing it and thinking about it for long periods of time until we wonder why we are feeling down. Or, by endlessly having others pray over our hurt and emotions while we continue to rehearse our pain. Yet God wants us free so we can freely love.

We ask people for a testimony after they have been prayed for and they often mention they have forgiven someone who hurt them deeply. Personally, it's amazing to see so many people being set free today. Jesus was delivering His people when He walked the earth. Today He is still delivering His people. He is looking for us to partner with His Holy Spirit to set His people free. He is coming for a spotless bride. How very merciful is our God.

He Wants to Walk You to Your Miracle

You ask for a breakthrough, but God may give you instructions. You ask for your healing, but Jesus may ask you a question. You want a miracle, but heaven will dig deeper to get to your heart. The means to your miracle may not be what you think.

Scripture is full of examples of people imploring God for miracles. And yet, the way they received their miracle was rarely what they expected. Consider these Biblical examples that reveal how God's priority is something much deeper than just a miracle:

- Naaman expected the prophet to wave his hand and declare him healed. Instead, he was told, "Go dip in the Jordan seven times and you will be clean." Initially complaining, he finally relented, and once he followed the instruction, he came out of the waters healed. (2 Kings 5:8-14)

  Naaman was after his healing, but GOD WAS AFTER NAAMAN'S PRIDE.

- Abraham expected his wife to get pregnant while still physically able. God purposely waited until it was impossible – and then planted the seed. (Genesis 21:1-7)

  Abraham was seeking an heir, but GOD WAS SEEKING ABRAHAM'S TRUST.

- Moses presumed upon previous experience to get water out of a rock. But God's instruction changed, and Moses paid the price for not listening. (Numbers 20:7-11)

  Moses was after miraculous provision, but GOD WAS AFTER MOSES' OBEDIENCE.

- Two blind men cried out for mercy to receive their sight, and Jesus asked them a question. Upon their declaration of faith, they were healed. (Matthew 9:27-31)

The blind men wanted to see, but JESUS WANTED THEIR CONFESSION.

- The invalid in Bethesda expected his healing to come by entering the waters at the pool. But Jesus told him to "Get up, pick up your mat, and walk." When he did, the man was healed. (John 5:2-9)

  The lame man just wanted to walk again, but JESUS WANTED HIM TO TAKE RESPONSIBILITY.

- When the ten lepers came to Jesus for healing, He told them, "Go show yourselves to the priests." As they were going, they were instantly healed. (Luke 17:14)

  The lepers wanted to be clean, but JESUS WANTED THEM FREE FROM CONDEMNATION.

- Friends brought Jesus a blind man, wanting a simple touch to heal him. Jesus took the man outside the village, spit on his eyes, and prayed two times before the man was healed. (Mark 8:22-26)

  The friends wanted a simple touch of healing, but JESUS WANTED TO MINISTER TO THE MAN.

- When Bartimaeus the blind beggar cried out for mercy, Jesus asked him what he wanted. When he requested his sight, Jesus healed him. (Mark 10:46-54)

  Bartimaeus wanted his sight, but JESUS WANTED HIS FAITH.

- Knowing that Lazarus was dying, his sisters sent for Jesus to come and heal him. Jesus waited until Lazarus was dead, and then rose him up from the grave. (John 11:1-44)

  The sisters wanted divine intervention, but JESUS FORESHADOWED HIS OWN RESURRECTION.

Throughout the majority of miracles recorded in Scripture, God's responses were rarely instantaneous. Rather, He always dug deeper to ask probing questions and challenge peoples' faith. Why? Because He is not satisfied in being our Miracle Maker. He wants to be Lord. He longs for us to seek Him on a continual basis and not merely presume upon His power.

Decreeing and declaring God's promises has its place, but it should never replace a sensitivity to His voice and a willingness to change course on the journey. In many of these examples, God was not focused on their breakthrough, but was looking to establish their faith, deepen their love, and build them up as mighty warriors for His purpose. The miracles simply followed as the result of their obedience.

When we allow Him to walk us to our miracle, we are shown His true nature and a depth of fellowship that is otherwise inaccessible. He may not give us our breakthrough on a silver platter, but He will refine our hearts as pure gold. He will use our need as a means to a greater end. Because in seeking our miracle, we will end up finding Him, and that's the breakthrough HE'S looking for.

NOTES

How Jesus Healed:

How the Disciples and the Apostles Healed

Here is a brief overview of the patterns and practices for healing found in the New Testament. These scriptures are cited from the English Standard Version

How Jesus Healed

He healed every disease.
And He went throughout all Galilee, teaching in their synagogues and proclaiming the gospel of the kingdom and healing every disease and every affliction among the people. (Matthew 4:23)

He touched the man and spoke the word.
And behold, a leper came to Him and knelt before Him, saying, "Lord, if You will, You can make me clean." And Jesus stretched out His hand and touched him, saying, "I will; be clean." And immediately his leprosy was cleansed. (Matthew 8:2-3, Mark 1:40-42, Luke 5:12-13)

He spoke the word from a distance.
Lord, my servant is lying paralyzed at home, suffering terribly." And He said to him, "I will come and heal him." But the centurion replied, "Lord, I am not worthy to have You come under my roof, but only say the word, and my servant will be healed. For, I too, am a man under authority, with soldiers under me. And I say to one, 'Go,' and he goes, and to another, 'Come,' and he comes, and to my servant, 'Do this,' and he does it." When Jesus heard this, He marveled and said to those who followed Him, "Truly, I tell you, with no one in Israel have I found such faith. I tell you, many will come from east and west and recline at table with Abraham, Isaac, and Jacob in the kingdom of heaven, while the sons of the kingdom will be thrown into the outer darkness. In that place there will be weeping and gnashing of teeth." And to the centurion Jesus said, "Go; let it be done for you as you have believed." And the servant was healed at that very moment. (Matthew 8:6-13, Luke 7:2-10)

He touched her hand.
And when Jesus entered Peter's house, He saw his mother-in-law lying sick with a fever. He touched her hand, and the fever left her, and she rose and began to serve Him. (Matthew 8:14-15, Mark 1:30-31, Luke 4:38-39)

He healed all who were sick.
That evening they brought to Him many who were oppressed by demons, and He cast out the spirits with a word and healed all who were sick. (Matthew 8:16, Mark 1:34)

He brought deliverance first.
And the demons begged Him, saying, "If You cast us out, send us away into the herd of pigs." And He said to them, "Go." So they came out and went into the pigs, and behold, the whole herd rushed down the steep bank into the sea and drowned in the waters. (Matthew 8:31-32) (compare with Luke 8:28-33)

He extended healing just as easily as extending forgiveness.
And behold, some people brought to Him a paralytic, lying on a bed. And when Jesus saw their faith, He said to the paralytic, "Take heart, My son; your sins are forgiven." And behold, some of the scribes said to themselves, "This man is blaspheming." But Jesus, knowing their thoughts, said, "Why do you think evil in your hearts? For which is easier, to say, 'Your sins are forgiven,' or to say, 'Rise and walk'? But that you may know that the Son of Man has authority on earth to forgive sins" - He then said to the paralytic - "Rise, pick up your bed and go home." And he rose and went home. (Matthew 9:2-7, Mark 2:5-10, Luke 5:18-25)

He cited personal faith in being made well.
And behold, a woman who had suffered from a discharge of blood for twelve years came up behind Him and touched the fringe of His garment, for she said to herself, "If I only touch His garment, I will be made well." Jesus turned, and seeing her He said, "Take heart, daughter; your faith has made you well." And instantly the woman was made well. (Matthew 9:20-22, Mark 5:27-34, Luke 8:43-48)

He spoke no words – simply rose the girl up.
He said, "Go away, for the girl is not dead but sleeping." And they laughed at Him. But when the crowd had been put outside, He went in and took her by the hand, and the girl arose. (Matthew 9:24-25) (compare with Mark 5:41-42 and Luke 8:49-55)

He touched their eyes and spoke an affirmation of their faith.
When He entered the house, the blind men came to Him, and Jesus said to them, "Do you believe that I am able to do this?" They said to Him, "Yes, Lord." Then He touched their eyes, saying, "According to your faith be it done to you." And their eyes were opened. And Jesus sternly warned them, "See that no one knows about it." (Matthew 9:28-30)

He brought deliverance, which brought the healing.
As they were going away, behold, a demon-oppressed man who was mute was brought to Him. And when the demon had been cast out, the mute man spoke. And the crowds marveled, saying, "Never was anything like this seen in Israel." (Matthew 9:32-33)

He gave authority to others.
And He called to Him His twelve disciples and gave them authority over unclean spirits, to cast them out, and to heal every disease and every affliction. (Matthew 10:1)

He spoke a simple command.
Then He said to the man, "Stretch out your hand." And the man stretched it out, and it was restored, healthy like the other. (Matthew 12:13, Mark 3:3-5, Luke 6:8-10)

He healed all who followed Him.
Jesus, aware of this, withdrew from there. And many followed Him, and He healed them all. (Matthew 12:15, Luke 6:17-19)

He healed a man whose sickness was caused by demons.

Then a demon-oppressed man who was blind and mute was brought to Him, and He healed him, so that the man spoke and saw. (Matthew 12:22)

His compassion stirred healing power.

When He went ashore He saw a great crowd, and He had compassion on them and healed their sick. (Matthew 14:14)

His garment was touched.

And when the men of that place recognized Him, they sent around to all that region and brought to Him all who were sick and implored Him that they might only touch the fringe of His garment. And as many as touched it were made well. (Matthew 14:35-36, Mark 6:56)

He healed the girl made sick by demonic oppression.

And behold, a Canaanite woman from that region came out and was crying, "Have mercy on me, O Lord, Son of David; my daughter is severely oppressed by a demon."... Then Jesus answered her, "O woman, great is your faith! Be it done for you as you desire." And her daughter was healed instantly. (Matthew 15:22, 28)

He asked a question provoking an affirmation of faith.

And stopping, Jesus called them and said, "What do you want Me to do for you?" They said to Him, "Lord, let our eyes be opened." And Jesus in pity touched their eyes, and immediately they recovered their sight and followed Him. (Matthew 20:32-34)

He spoke a word to raise the dead.

Taking her by the hand He said to her, "Talitha cumi," which means, "Little girl, I say to you, arise." And immediately the girl got up and began walking (for she was twelve years of age), and they were immediately overcome with amazement. (Mark 5:41-42)

He saw corporate unbelief limit miracles.

And Jesus said to them, "A prophet is not without honor, except in his hometown and among his relatives and in his own household." And He could do no mighty work there, except that He laid His hands on a few sick people and healed them. And He marveled because of their unbelief. (Mark 6:4-6)

He did prophetic actions and gave the command.
And they brought to Him a man who was deaf and had a speech impediment, and they begged Him to lay His hand on him. And taking him aside from the crowd privately, He put His fingers into his ears, and after spitting touched his tongue. And looking up to heaven, He sighed and said to him, "Ephphatha," that is, "Be opened." And his ears were opened, his tongue was released, and he spoke plainly. (Mark 7:32-35)

He conferred with the man and prayed more than once.
And He took the blind man by the hand and led him out of the village, and when He had spit on his eyes and laid His hands on him, He asked him, "Do you see anything?" And he looked up and said, "I see people, but they look like trees, walking." Then Jesus laid His hands on his eyes again; and he opened his eyes, his sight was restored, and he saw everything clearly. And He sent him to his home, saying, "Do not even enter the village." (Mark 8:23-26)

He rebuked a demon and mentioned prayer and fasting as a factor.
And when Jesus saw that a crowd came running together, He rebuked the unclean spirit, saying to it, "You mute and deaf spirit, I command you, come out of him and never enter him again." And after crying out and convulsing him terribly, it came out, and the boy was like a corpse, so that most of them said, "He is dead." But Jesus took him by the hand and lifted him up, and he arose. And when He had entered the house, His disciples asked Him privately, "Why could we not cast it out?" And He said to them, "This kind cannot be driven out by anything but prayer." (Mark 9:25-29) (compare with Matthew 17:18-21 and Luke 9:39-42)

He asked a question to provoke faith.
And Jesus stopped and said, "Call him." And they called the blind man, saying to him, "Take heart. Get up; He is calling you." And throwing off his cloak, he sprang up and came to Jesus. And Jesus said to him, "What do you want Me to do for you?" And the blind man said to Him, "Rabbi,

let me recover my sight." And Jesus said to him, "Go your way; your faith has made you well." And immediately he recovered his sight and followed Him on the way. (Mark 10:49-52, Luke 18:38-43)

He imparted healing through touch.
And all the crowd sought to touch Him, for power came out from Him and healed them all. (Luke 6:19)

His compassion was followed by a touch which raised the dead.
And when the Lord saw her, He had compassion on her and said to her, "Do not weep." Then He came up and touched the bier, and the bearers stood still. And He said, "Young man, I say to you, arise." And the dead man sat up and began to speak, and Jesus gave him to his mother. (Luke 7:13-15)

He brought deliverance, then healing.
When he saw Jesus, he cried out and fell down before Him and said with a loud voice, "What have You to do with me, Jesus, Son of the Most High God? I beg You, do not torment me." For He had commanded the unclean spirit to come out of the man. (For many a time it had seized him. He was kept under guard and bound with chains and shackles, but he would break the bonds and be driven by the demon into the desert.) Jesus then asked him, "What is your name?" And he said, "Legion," for many demons had entered him. And they begged Him not to command them to depart into the abyss. Now a large herd of pigs was feeding there on the hillside, and they begged Him to let them enter these. So He gave them permission. Then the demons came out of the man and entered the pigs, and the herd rushed down the steep bank into the lake and drowned. (Luke 8:28-33)

He spoke encouragement to believe and to be free from fear.
While He was still speaking, someone from the ruler's house came and said, "Your daughter is dead; do not trouble the Teacher any more." But Jesus on hearing this answered him, "Do not fear; only believe, and she will be well." And when He came to the house, He allowed no one to enter with Him, except Peter and John and James, and the father and mother of the child. And all were weeping and mourning for her, but He said, "Do not weep, for she is not dead but sleeping." And they laughed at Him, knowing

that she was dead. But taking her by the hand He called, saying, "Child, arise." (Luke 8:49-54)

He spoke freedom from disability then laid hands on her.

And behold, there was a woman who had had a disabling spirit for eighteen years. She was bent over and could not fully straighten herself. When Jesus saw her, He called her over and said to her, "Woman, you are freed from your disability." And He laid his hands on her, and immediately she was made straight, and she glorified God. (Luke 13:11-13)

He took the man (spoke no words?)

And behold, there was a man before Him who had dropsy. And Jesus responded to the lawyers and Pharisees, saying, "Is it lawful to heal on the Sabbath, or not?" But they remained silent. Then He took him and healed him and sent him away. (Luke 14:2-4)

He gave a directive, and healing came as they obeyed.

And as He entered a village, He was met by ten lepers, who stood at a distance and lifted up their voices, saying, "Jesus, Master, have mercy on us." When He saw them, He said to them, "Go and show yourselves to the priests." And as they went, they were cleansed. (Luke 17:12-14)

He pronounced "life." The fever left, but recovery was still needed.

When this man heard that Jesus had come from Judea to Galilee, he went to Him and asked Him to come down and heal his son, for he was at the point of death. So Jesus said to him, "Unless you see signs and wonders you will not believe." The official said to Him, "Sir, come down before my child dies." Jesus said to him, "Go; your son will live." The man believed the word that Jesus spoke to him and went on his way. As he was going down, his servants met him and told him that his son was recovering. So, he asked them the hour when he began to get better, and they said to him, "Yesterday at the seventh hour the fever left him." The father knew that was the hour when Jesus had said to him, "Your son will live." And he himself believed, and all his household. (John 4:47-53)

He focused on taking action – spoke to the roadblock in healing.
When Jesus saw him lying there and knew that he had already been there a long time, He said to him, "Do you want to be healed?" The sick man answered Him, "Sir, I have no one to put me into the pool when the water is stirred up, and while I am going another steps down before me." Jesus said to him, "Get up, take up your bed, and walk." And at once the man was healed, and he took up his bed and walked. (John 5:6-9)

He pointed to sin as a root of sickness.
Afterward, Jesus found him (paralytic healed at the pool) in the temple and said to him, "See, you are well! Sin no more, that nothing worse may happen to you." (John 5:14)

He gave a "treatment" and then a directive –
healing came upon obedience.
As He passed by, He saw a man blind from birth. And His disciples asked Him, "Rabbi, who sinned, this man or his parents, that he was born blind?" Jesus answered, "It was not that this man sinned, or his parents, but that the works of God might be displayed in him. We must work the works of Him who sent me while it is day; night is coming, when no one can work. As long as I am in the world, I am the light of the world." Having said these things, He spit on the ground and made mud with the saliva. Then He anointed the man's eyes with the mud and said to him, "Go, wash in the pool of Siloam" (which means Sent). So, he went and washed and came back seeing. (John 9:1-7)

He gave a directive to test their faith and prayed openly
for the sake of witnesses.
The command was to "come out" (not just "be healed" or "rise up.")
Then Jesus, deeply moved again, came to the tomb. It was a cave, and a stone lay against it. Jesus said, "Take away the stone." Martha, the sister of the dead man, said to Him, "Lord, by this time there will be an odor, for he has been dead four days." Jesus said to her, "Did I not tell you that if you believed you would see the glory of God?" So, they took away the stone. And Jesus lifted up His eyes and said, "Father, I thank You that You have heard Me. I knew that You always hear Me, but I said this on account of

the people standing around, that they may believe that You sent Me." When He had said these things, He cried out with a loud voice, "Lazarus, come out." The man who had died came out, his hands and feet bound with linen strips, and his face wrapped with a cloth. Jesus said to them, "Unbind him, and let him go." (John 11:38-44)

How the Disciples and the Apostles Healed

Spoke to distraction, called for focus, gave the command and then helped him up.

And Peter directed his gaze at him, as did John, and said, "Look at us." And he fixed his attention on them, expecting to receive something from them. But Peter said, "I have no silver and gold, but what I do have I give to you. In the name of Jesus Christ of Nazareth, rise up and walk!" And he took him by the right hand and raised him up, and immediately his feet and ankles were made strong. And leaping up, he stood and began to walk, and entered the temple with them, walking, and leaping, and praising God. (Acts 3:4-8)

Healed by their shadows.

And more than ever believers were added to the Lord, multitudes of both men and women, so that they even carried out the sick into the streets and laid them on cots and mats, that as Peter came by at least his shadow might fall on some of them. The people also gathered from the towns around Jerusalem, bringing the sick and those afflicted with unclean spirits, and they were all healed. (Acts 5:14-16)

"Many" were healed instead of "all" – possibly because of Simon the sorcerer?

And the crowds with one accord paid attention to what was being said by Philip when they heard him and saw the signs that he did. For unclean spirits, crying out with a loud voice, came out of many who had them, and many who were paralyzed or lame were healed. (Acts 8:6-7)

Said "Jesus Christ heals you" – gave directive.

Now as Peter went here and there among them all, he came down also to the saints who lived at Lydda. There he found a man named Aeneas, bed-ridden for eight years, who was paralyzed. And Peter said to him, "Aeneas, Jesus Christ heals you; rise and make your bed." And immediately he rose. (Acts 9:32-34)

Followed Jesus' example.

So Peter rose and went with them. And when he arrived, they took him to the upper room. All the widows stood beside him weeping and showing tunics and other garments that Dorcas made while she was with them. But Peter put them all outside and knelt down and prayed; and turning to the body he said, "Tabitha, arise." And she opened her eyes, and when she saw Peter she sat up. And he gave her his hand and raised her up. Then calling the saints and widows, he presented her alive. (Acts 9:39-41)

Perceived faith and gave the command.

Now at Lystra there was a man sitting who could not use his feet. He was crippled from birth and had never walked. He listened to Paul speaking. And Paul, looking intently at him and seeing that he had faith to be made well, said in a loud voice, "Stand upright on your feet." And he sprang up and began walking. (Acts 14:8-10)

Garments carried healing power.

And God was doing extraordinary miracles by the hands of Paul, so that even handkerchiefs or aprons that had touched his skin were carried away to the sick, and their diseases left them and the evil spirits came out of them. (Acts 19:11-12)

Picked the man up and spoke life.

And a young man named Eutychus, sitting at the window, sank into a deep sleep as Paul talked still longer. And being overcome by sleep, he fell down from the third story and was taken up dead. But Paul went down and bent over him, and taking him in his arms, said, "Do not be alarmed, for his life is in him." And when Paul had gone up and had broken bread and eaten, he conversed with them a long while, until daybreak, and so departed. And they took the youth away alive, and were not a little comforted. (Acts 20:9-12)

Observations in how Jesus healed:

- Jesus commanded healing – He never asked for it.
- Several specific sicknesses/spirits mentioned: blindness, paralysis, issue of blood, leprosy, mute, speech impediment, crippled, bedridden, deafness, disabling spirit, unclean spirit, spirit of infirmity (in other translations).
- He healed both through WORDS as well as through TOUCH.
- He didn't always use the word "healing" but often spoke life and wellness.
- His compassion often directed miracles – especially raising from the dead.
- He often gave directives to follow in order for the healing to be complete.
- He looked for faith and often asked about a person's desire before responding.
- He approached each healing differently, based on the person's history and circumstance.
- He perceived when demonic interference was the cause of sickness and addressed that first.
- Some of the healings required action first and some involved gradual recovery after the initial breakthrough.
- His focus was consistently on their HEART before their healing – their physical healing would come as a result of their heart being healed

Summations:

Jesus' demonstrations of healing were to verify His identity as the Son of God, and His Father's will for complete healing and deliverance for all.

For the disciples/apostles, they followed Jesus' example. But the record shows more focus on declaring the Kingdom of God, with healing as a tool to build faith or validate their message. Miracles were not the focus – rather declaring the Kingdom of Christ (which brought miracles).

7-Day
Corporate Prayer for Healing

Gathering for an hour of prayer, for seven days, to prepare the way for healing.

Therefore, confess your sins to one another and pray for one another, that you may be healed. (James 5:15)

I believe the Lord is calling the Body of Christ to come together in prayer for the healing of bodies and souls. There are not only principalities of control and deception hovering over our regions and nations, but there are also principalities of sickness and disease. Until a greater authority from the unified Ecclesia arises, these strongholds and territorial spirits can rule over our communities and override our pleas for help. Spirits of infirmity are at work over many regions and the Lord is inviting us to defeat and displace these strongholds through corporate agreement and collective prayer.

This is the hour where "our" faith is critical. Not just "my" faith, or "your" faith, but "our" faith. If we are to see the strongholds of sickness and disease broken, we must come into agreement as the Body of Christ. James tells us that we should confess our sins to one another so that we may be healed. Matthew 18:19-20 teaches that the agreement of two or three draws the Father's ear and produces a fruitful outcome. Thus, in addition to faith, our healing can come as the result of mutual submission and oneness in prayer.

The following outline addresses some of the scriptural directives concerning healing. And though we can never "work" for our healing, it is clear that we can prepare the way. By addressing the following issues, we are asking for Holy Spirit to clear our hearts and minds of anything that may be standing in the way of God's healing grace and power. As we pray with others concerning these things, we are inviting Holy Spirit to reveal any strongholds at work or any areas of surrender that can better "make way" for Him to move on our behalf, both personally and corporately.

Fasting during this prayer initiative is subject to the Lord's direction for each participant. The focus is not giving up something during this seven-day period, but intentionally giving Him our full attention. Lastly, since the whole purpose of this initiative is to join with others in prayer, determine to make that effort and not simply pray alone. There are things the Lord will reveal and impart to us when we are together, that we will not receive when we pray alone. Let's celebrate this opportunity for fellowship and join together for our breakthrough.

But for you who fear my name, the sun of righteousness shall rise with healing in its wings. You shall go out leaping like calves from the stall. And you shall tread down the wicked, for they will be ashes under the soles of your feet, on the day when I act, says the Lord of hosts. (Malachi 4:2-3)

Day One

Discerning the Body

1 Corinthians 11:27-31

Whoever, therefore, eats the bread or drinks the cup of the Lord in an unworthy manner will be guilty concerning the body and blood of the Lord. Let a person examine himself, then, and so eat of the bread and drink of the cup. For anyone who eats and drinks without discerning the body eats and drinks judgment on himself. That is why many of you are weak and ill, and some have died. But if we judged ourselves truly, we would not be judged.

1. Reaffirm your belief in the power of Christ's blood to cleanse us from sin and restore us to a right relationship with Him.

2. Offer thanksgiving for the body and blood of our Lord, declaring His complete victory over sickness, disease, and every curse of the enemy. Acknowledge any area where you have trusted in your own resources and not applied the finished work of the cross.

3. Invite Holy Spirit to help you discern your own body. Consider the current state of your own spirit, soul, mind, and body. Repent for any way in which you have denied, refused, or ignored the Spirit's prompting concerning any unresolved issues in your life.

4. Invite Holy Spirit to help you better discern the Body of Christ and the health and well-being of your spiritual family. Repent for any self-preoccupation that has blinded you to the needs of those around you.

5. Ask for insights in how to pray for others in their healing journey.

Day Two

Renouncing Sexual Immorality and Idolatry

Revelation 2:20-22

But I have this against you, that you tolerate that woman Jezebel, who calls herself a prophetess and is teaching and seducing my servants to practice sexual immorality and to eat food sacrificed to idols. I gave her time to repent, but she refuses to repent of her sexual immorality. Behold, I will throw her onto a sickbed, and those who commit adultery with her I will throw into great tribulation, unless they repent of her works.

1. Worship the Lord in the beauty of His holiness. Thank Him for extending holiness to us as we take on His nature and character. (1 Peter 1:16-17)

2. Ask Holy Spirit to open your eyes to any sexual sin or moral compromise in your own life. Repent for any way in which you have overlooked or tolerated any unhealthy practices that have compromised God's standard for holiness.

3. Repent of and renounce any and all forms of sexual immorality in the congregation, including pornography, sexting, chat rooms, or any kind of sexual perversion. Repent for looking at or viewing online movies or shows that are inappropriate or graphic. Reaffirm your desire to guard your eyes and ears from fleshly temptations and the enemy's traps.

4. Repent for allowing or tolerating influence from others in your life who are walking in compromise and drawing you away from God's standards for purity.

5. Repent for the collective ignorance and unbelief concerning sexual immorality inside the Church at large. As exposures of high-profile ministers continue to emerge, pray for a cleansing of the pulpits and a sanctification of the saints.

6. Affirm a personal and collective conviction in walking in holiness and freedom, determining to speak and act in a way that honors the Lord and one another.

Day Three

Getting Free from Offense and Roots of Bitterness

Hebrews 12:12-17

Therefore lift your drooping hands and strengthen your weak knees, and make straight paths for your feet, so that what is lame may not be put out of joint but rather be healed. Strive for peace with everyone, and for the holiness without which no one will see the Lord. See to it that no one fails to obtain the grace of God; that no "root of bitterness" springs up and causes trouble, and by it many become defiled; that no one is sexually immoral or unholy like Esau, who sold his birthright for a single meal. For you know that afterward, when he desired to inherit the blessing, he was rejected, for he found no chance to repent, though he sought it with tears.

1. Declare your desire to live in peace with others and be free of any offense, either personal or corporate.

2. Invite Holy Spirit to reveal any area of unforgiveness or any relationship that needs reconciliation. Forgive and release those who have hurt you or disappointed you and bless those who have spoken ill of you. Release any bitterness of soul, uproot any seed of resentment, and invite Holy Spirit to cleanse you of all toxic emotions.

3. Pray that those who have been wounded by the Church will find healing, deliverance, and freedom from the past. Pray that prodigals will return, and the lost will find a place to call home.

4. Invite Holy Spirit to do a cleansing work in the congregation so that each member will be built up in sincere love for one another, free from offense or strife.

Day Four

Getting Free from Disappointments, Depression, and Oppression

Proverbs 13:12
Hope deferred makes the heart sick, but a desire fulfilled is a tree of life.

Proverbs 16:24
Gracious words are like a honeycomb, sweetness to the soul and health to the body.

Proverbs 17:22
A joyful heart is good medicine, but a crushed spirit dries up the bones.

1. Praise God for the life-giving power of His Word to bring healing and hope.

2. Ask Holy Spirit to reveal any personal areas of hope deferred or disappointment and invite the Lord to heal the wounds and bring fresh perspective to pains from the past.

3. Speak to any spirits of depression or oppression, both personally and corporately, by declaring hope and a bright future.

4. Break off any word curses by speaking words of truth, love, and power.

5. Declare a fresh joy of the Lord to be released to displace the yoke of heaviness

Day Five

Declaring Obedience to His Word and Voice

Exodus 15:26

Saying, "If you will diligently listen to the voice of the Lord your God, and do that which is right in his eyes, and give ear to his commandments and keep all his statutes, I will put none of the diseases on you that I put on the Egyptians, for I am the Lord, your healer."

Exodus 23:25

You shall serve the Lord your God, and he will bless your bread and your water, and I will take sickness away from among you.

Proverbs 4:20-22

My son, be attentive to my words; incline your ear to my sayings. Let them not escape from your sight; keep them within your heart. For they are life to those who find them, and healing to all their flesh.

1. Declare your intent to listen to the voice of the Lord and do what is right in His eyes. Repent for any way in which you have personally not obeyed His voice or kept His Word.

2. Acknowledge a lack of understanding concerning the toxic and dangerous effects of various foods and drugs that have made us sick. Repent for any addictions to food or drugs and ask the Holy Spirit to teach us how to rightly care for our bodies.

3. Reaffirm our collective desire to obey His Word and pray that we will keep in step with His directives.

4. Speak blessing on the teaching of the Word in the congregation. Pray that we will be doers of the Word and not merely listeners.

Day Six

Ministering to those Bound and Broken

Isaiah 58:6-8

Is not this the fast that I choose: to loose the bonds of wickedness, to undo the straps of the yoke, to let the oppressed go free, and to break every yoke? Is it not to share your bread with the hungry and bring the homeless poor into your house; when you see the naked, to cover him, and not to hide yourself from your own flesh? Then shall your light break forth like the dawn, and your healing shall spring up speedily; your righteousness shall go before you; the glory of the LORD shall be your rear guard.

1. Thank the Lord for the abundance of His House and all that He provides.

2. Affirm our desire to serve others out of sincere love and minister to those in need.

3. Repent for ways in which we have personally or collectively ignored the needs of others or missed God's invitation to help. Ask the Lord to open our eyes to the hurting and be attentive to those who need care.

4. Pray that we would be a House of healing as well as a House of provision. Pray that we would become conduits of the Father's blessings.

Day Seven
Praying for Our Leaders

Deuteronomy 5:16
Honor your father and your mother, as the Lord your God commanded you, that your days may be long, and that it may go well with you in the land that the Lord your God is giving you.

Acts 28:7-10
Now in the neighborhood of that place were lands belonging to the chief man of the island, named Publius, who received us and entertained us hospitably for three days. It happened that the father of Publius lay sick with fever and dysentery. And Paul visited him and prayed, and putting his hands on him, healed him. And when this had taken place, the rest of the people on the island who had diseases also came and were cured. They also honored us greatly, and when we were about to sail, they put on board whatever we needed.

1. Pray for and bless the spiritual fathers and mothers, both in the home and the Church.

2. Repent for any ill words or thoughts towards those in positions of spiritual authority, both inside the Church and out.

3. Pray for the apostles and prophets who help lay the spiritual foundations and are set apart to model Kingdom authority (Eph 2:20). Pray that authentic signs, wonders, and miracles would follow those whom the Lord has called and appointed in this hour.

4. Pray that influential leaders and community gatekeepers would be touched by God's healing power and break open entire regions for miracles and breakthroughs.

5. Pray that godly leadership would rise and take root in the community and the nation so that Kingdom authority will overtake the works of darkness.

About the Author

Wanda has been in ministry for over 35 years as a worship leader, teacher, author, deliverance counselor, and speaker. She is an ordained minister, commissioned fivefold leader, and passionate about interpreting life from heaven's perspective. Since an unexpected angelic encounter in 2002, Wanda ministers through a spirit of wisdom and revelation that empowers believers to know their authority, embrace their calling, and demonstrate heavenly realities on the earth (Ephesians 1:17).

She has written seven books as well as numerous videos and audio teaching series which are available through her website (wandaalger.me) and Amazon. She writes weekly blog posts in addition to video podcasts on both YouTube and Rumble. You can also find her on most social media platforms.

She is married to Bobby Alger, Lead Pastor of Crossroads Community Church in Winchester, Virginia which they founded together in 1998. They have three grown children and a growing number of grandchildren.

VISIT WANDA'S WEBSITE at wandaalger.me where you can find her latest articles, prophetic words, and videos, in addition to all her teaching resources, prayer guides, and an online library of topical studies for further research and prayer.

Made in the USA
Middletown, DE
01 November 2024